for Jesus! Stay Close to Him!

Rick Barton

Rom 15:13

God on the Fireline
A Firefighter's Journal

Rick Barton

PUBLISHED BY

Rick Barton Ministries

God on the Fireline: *A Firefighter's Journal*

Published by Rick Barton Ministries
PO Box 1155, Gunnison, CO 81230

ISBN: 978-1721672868

Cover design by LaVonne Ewing

*To my wife Melva
and our children, Joy, Rebekah, Steve and Tim*

ON THE COVER

I call this picture, Dropping on the Rat. I took it while serving as Safety Officer on the Rat Creek Fire near Wisdom, Montana. As the sun began to set, the Division Supervisor and I watched a helicopter making water drops. It was definitely a "God moment" as we marveled at His power and the beauty of His creation. Later, when I wrote the Wildland Firefighter's 23rd Psalm I thought the two seemed to fit together.

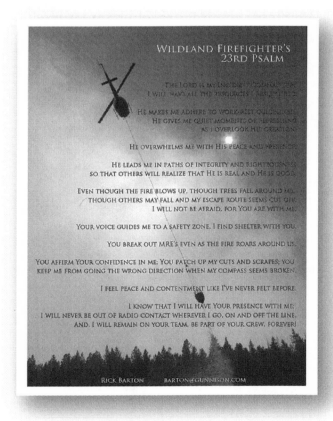

The Wildland Firefighter's 23rd Psalm poster (18x24)

Wildland Firefighter's 23rd Psalm

by Rick Barton

The Lord is my Incident Commander
I will have all the resources I will really need.

He makes me adhere to work-rest guidelines:
He gives me quiet moments of refreshing
As I overlook His creation.

He overwhelms me with His peace and presence.

He leads in paths of integrity and righteousness
So that others will realize that He is real and He is good.

Even though the fire blows up, though trees fall around me
Though others may fall and my escape route seems cut off,
I will not be afraid, for You are with me.

Your voice guides me to a safety zone;
I find my shelter with You.

You break out MRE's even as the fire roars around us.

You affirm Your confidence in me; You patch up my cuts
and scrapes; You keep me from going the wrong direction
when my compass seems broken.

I feel peace and contentment like I've never felt before.

I know that I will have Your presence with me; I will never
be out of radio contact wherever I go, on and off the line.
And, I will remain on your team, be part of Your crew,
forever!

Contents

Chapter – The Armor of God

Chapter 4 – Witnessing

Chapter Five – Temptation

Chapter Six – Encouragment

Chapter Seven – A Time for Laughter

Chapter Eight – God of Grace

Chapter Nine – Lessons Learned on the Fireline

Chapter Ten – Believe and Receive

Fireplace Fodder Song

God Must Be a Firefighter at Heart

Have you ever sat around a fire camp and enjoyed fellowship with your fellow firefighters? Maybe someone picked up a guitar for some singing. There's nothing like music to calm the heart. If such an opportunity presents itself, here's a "Wildland Melody" I put together to the tune of *God Must Be a Cowboy at Heart*.

Campfire coffee, and an MRE in hand, double
bagged for sleeping when it's cold.
Punching in some fireline, Pulaski in my
hand, makes me long to see the ones I love.

Coming in to fire camp, is a lot like coming home,
friends and loved ones always seem to show.
We've faced hardships together, hunkered down at
times, when that crazy fire began to blow.

And I think God must be a firefighter at heart.
He made large plumes and columns from the start.
He made sage and manzanita, eucalyptus and oak
brush, and Santa Ana winds all in a rush.

The bright lights of the city, don't do so much for
me. You only spend your pay and all your H.
I'd rather walk with Jesus, out on this mountain top,
and marvel at its beauty and His grace.

Fourteen days seem too many, other times too few.
It all depends on what's happening at home.

There's bills to pay and mouths to feed, and calls to
answer too, maybe an extension, not too long.

When I pull into the driveway, and see my loving
wife, and feel the tug of little hands in mine.

I'm glad this one is over, and ready for some time,
to rest and love and play a game or two.

Introduction

"This Is Dispatch;
We Have an Assignment for You"

Those words, or something very similar, cause the heart of every wildland firefighter to beat a little faster. It also starts a new adventure or chapter in our life. Whether we're a smokejumper, hotshot, engine or hand-crew member, we're part of a unique group of men and women. We might be volunteers called away from job and family, or professional smokechasers who actually look forward to 100-hour workweeks, sleeping in the dirt, eating out of a box and breathing smoke. It doesn't matter. We're all firefighters.

My first exposure to wildland fires[1] was as an 18-year-old straight out of high school. I had left my home in the city and gone to work on a ranch. After a few weeks I discovered that ranch work wasn't riding horses all day singing Yippee Yi Yo to a bunch of cows. In fact, I rarely even saw a horse. So, I walked into the Idlewild Ranger Station[2] and asked if they needed any help. The man at the desk looked at me amusedly, you have to apply in December and this was June, then thought again and hired me on the spot. The day before, two members of a trail crew had quit and they needed a fill-in right away. I had a day of training including how to dig a fire line and spent the summer camping out on beaver ponds building trails. When fall came I headed to Gunnison, CO to attend college. Shortly after classes began, two large fires broke out nearby and they offered to pay any students who

---

[1] "Wildland" is term that designates forest, brush or grass fires as opposed to "Urban" or structure fires in communities. The term "Urban Interface" is one we use to describe a wildland fire that's entered an urban setting or vice-versa.
[2] A United States Forest Service Ranger Station near Winter Park, CO now closed.

wanted to work.[3] And, the college Dean gave excuses for classes missed! Signing up as quick as I could I spent several days carrying water up steep hillsides to support fire crews who were brought in to suppress the fire. I almost passed out from exhaustion but the exhilaration, extreme work, and camaraderie I sensed, made me want more.

Now, after five decades, I still love it! One day someone asked me why I enjoyed fire assignments so much. I was about to answer something about "H's" and "O's" (hazard and overtime pay) but another firefighter really nailed the answer. He said, "It's not about the money, it's about the feeling you get as a member of a very special team. You face danger and hardship together as well as long periods away from home in difficult circumstances. After a while you realize you've become part of a family and every fire becomes a family reunion." He was right.

This book is a collection of my screw-ups, near misses and the occasional times I got it right. Some of my co-workers might remember the time I took a fire engine 40 miles into the woods to a fire and forgot to fill it with water. They also wonder if I ever told the boss. Each story is true and written to encourage others as they go through their own fires in life. You'll find that as I learned to lean upon my Incident Commander, Jesus Christ, my love for what I do developed even more meaning and fulfillment.

The stories were originally published in *The Encourager* a magazine produced by the Fellowship of Christian Firefighters[4] (FCF). It is dedicated to my wife of nearly 50 years, Melva and our children, Joy, Rebekah, Steve and Tim, who supported me as I would dash off from the dinner table, sometimes to be gone for up to a month. Special thanks to Gay and Sue Reynolds, retired fire chief, and former Missionaries with the FCF who patiently gathered and edited the stories. *Soli Deo Gloria!*

---

[3] This no longer happens. Now you have to complete 40 hours of training and be certified to work on the fireline. This was 1967.

[4] The Fellowship of Christian Firefighters webpage: Fellowshipofchristianfire fighters.org or email: FCFmissionary@gmail.com

CHAPTER ONE

Priorities

Establishing What's Important

"He answered, 'Love the Lord your God with all your heart and with all your soul and with all your strength and with all your mind; and, 'Love your neighbor as yourself.'"

Luke 10:27

What's So "Happy" About a New Year?

"What day is it?" Ever asked that question? Have you noticed how on a busy incident, hours and days seem to run together? Important things such as your anniversary, birthdays, dentist appointments and even days of worship sneak up and sometimes slip by us.

That's one of the reasons I like ringing in the New Year. It forces me to stop the clock, gives me a chance to review the past year, and plan some goals for the new one.

How was your past year? Did you accomplish the things you set out to do? Did you get the garage painted? Take that long overdue vacation? Lose the twenty pounds? Or, even more importantly, did you spend time in your Bible each day, mend that broken relationship, and devote more quality time to your spouse and kids?

The New Year is a great time for reflection and goal setting. But don't wait for January to come around. Start now as you read this book. As some sage said, "If you fail to plan, you plan to fail." By writing down a list of goals, we can begin moving forward instead of just treading water or reacting to daily "emergencies." Sure, we may not reach all our goals right off, but we can reach some and that's a good start. It seems popular to discount "New Year's Resolutions" as being a waste of time. But is it?

What would you really like to see happen this year? Write it down. (I do it with my wife over a lunch out.) Then, post the list somewhere you'll see it often.

Start with your spiritual goals. Maybe you could start with reading through a *One Year Bible*. How about setting aside a regular time for prayer each day?

Or consider joining a small group or Bible study if you haven't already.

Now, write out your family goals. They might include: Having a date night with your spouse once a week? Or maybe planning that honeymoon you never had, or a second one? Taking a trip with your boys, girls, or parents?

Financial goals would be a good category to list. A great goal would be to get out of debt – starting with your credit cards – and perhaps getting financial counseling to help. Increase your giving to your church. Start a savings account for vacations or school expenses. And don't forget the household goals your spouse may have; a new window, painting the garage, etc.

All of these are achievable goals if you commit them to the Lord Jesus! (Psalm 37:5). And even if you don't reach them all this year, they become part of your long-range thinking. And, at the end of the year, review your list. I'll bet you'll do better than you think.

Why not use New Years for something more than party hats? You don't look so hot in one anyway, nor do I. Make your whole upcoming year a "Happy" one!

†

Blow Up

It was a wilderness fire gone bad. We had already lost one resort and the fire was lining up for its next meal!

Ignited by lightning weeks before, it had crept around, consuming years of accumulated dead and down trees. A small team of fire personnel monitored the fire's growth, pleased with how creation was restoring itself.

Then the winds came. The Weather Service issued its daily forecast, but this time it included a warning for strong and erratic winds. In the afternoon the winds hit and before responding units could deploy, the fire blew out of the wilderness and destroyed a popular and historic resort.

It would take months and even years to fully restore the resort. In the meantime, its workers set up a temporary kitchen and rented out their few remaining cabins to fire crews trying to contain the fire.

As we worked the fire, a crewmember turned to me and asked, "Can I talk to you about my marriage?" It seemed some of the same problems that had occurred on the fire had begun to show up in his home.

First, he and his wife had allowed several years of "dead and down" issues to accumulate. Instead of removing these to "God's burn pile" of confession, repentance and forgiveness, they had let them lay there, slowly piling up, a tinder box just waiting for a spark and some wind. And of course, the devil is always happy to provide a spark of contention and the wind of love-less words.

They ignored God's instruction to "not let the sun go down on your anger, and do not give the devil an opportunity" (Ephesians 4:26-27 NASB). This is tough, but asking forgiveness before we go to bed is a great start, even if we think we were "right." God also says "if you forgive others their transgressions, your heavenly Father will also forgive you. But if you do not forgive others, then your Father will not forgive your transgressions" (Matthew 6:14-15 NASB). Even if our spouse doesn't ask for forgiveness, we need to forgive them, right away. Ouch, that's a tough one! But if we don't obey God's directions, the fires come.

Second, instead of actively suppressing the "fire" through prayer, communication and counseling, they just tried to "monitor" their marriage. When we don't take aggressive action toward building a fireline around our problems and extinguishing them, we are taking the chance that a sudden burst of wind will cause a "blow-up" in our home. We have to take this seriously! "Line construction" will mean realigning our schedule to include our spouse and children in meaningful ways. It means planning our days off around our family's needs and wants, rather than our own. And most of all, putting Jesus at the center of our home!

This firefighter needed to initiate mop-up and prevention. Every firefighter knows that a key element of suppression is making sure the fire doesn't reignite. In our marriage this includes praying with our spouse and children, reading God's Word together, and consistent fellowship in a good church. If our schedule makes church times sporadic, we need to ask the pastor if there are applicable support groups that provide Bible study and fellowship opportunities for us and our spouse as a supplement.

In pre-cell phone days, prevention included standing in line up to an hour to use a pay phone. We were usually limited to three minutes, just enough time to tell my wife and kids that I loved them, as well as let them know where I was and how I was doing. Today it means once a day cell phone calls. On local fires it means calling my wife and telling her I'll be late, so she doesn't worry.

If the fire has already "blown up," causing hurt to our family; we have to look at two time-frames for recovery. In the *short-term* we have to keep on "cooking." Don't give up! It starts with serving our spouse and children as best we can. We must show as well as tell them that we've made mistakes and want to rectify them. We must not blame them; instead, ask God to help us work through the shortcomings in our life and attitude. In the *long-term*, we have to be patient. It can take months and even years of rebuilding the trust and love that was destroyed in a few hours. It's important to remember that our spouse isn't the problem, the devil is. Satan desires to steal, kill and destroy our families and our witness (Eph. 6:12-18, John 10:10). We must attack him, not our spouse! When we do, God will give us victory (James 4:7).

The difference we have as followers of Jesus is that we have the Holy Spirit. He is our lookout before things go bad, showing us "Situations that Shout Watch Out" in our family. This comes as we read God's Word, listen to our family and pray. He is our teacher and helper as we remove dead and down issues. He will help us rebuild our relationships as we trust and obey Him. Each day we should ask the Lord to fill us afresh with His Holy Spirit and help us to make our marriages fireproof. Families do matter to God!

That night in fire camp we held a short chapel service, prayed and looked at God's Word concerning the blessing of marriage. As we finished, we recommitted ourselves and our marriages to Jesus; that with His help we would clear out the "dead and down" issues and make way for fresh, new growth!

†

How Much Is Your Career Worth?

I was on a fire assignment in South Dakota. During a break, the conversation turned to a couple who had recently divorced because of infidelity by a woman involved in the fire service. The man who was talking "bragged" that he was responsible because he had introduced her to the other man. My heart was grieved, I knew the woman; she was a professing Christian. All I could blurt out to the speaker was, "how sad"!

Questions bombarded my mind. How could this happen? Why would a Christian woman throw aside her vow to God, vow to her husband and consequently destroy her family for an adulterous relationship? I felt betrayed as well. There are precious few believers in the fire community and one had just allowed the name of Jesus and the witness of all of us to be mocked by her actions.

After my feelings subsided, I began to think of other adulterous relationships I had observed on fire assignments. It seemed obvious that these marriages were experiencing problems at home before coming to the fire. Instead of staying at home and working on strengthening their marriage, they let their job in fire become an "escape," setting themselves up for the devil's snares and moral failure (2 Timothy 2:24-26).

To paraphrase Jesus, "What good does it do a firefighter to make lots of overtime and hazard pay, yet lose their own family and relationship with God?" (Luke 9:25, "Barton Edition"). Put another way; are your career, status, or fire qualifications worth disobeying God and bringing shame to your Savior's Name? Proverbs gives us a sad illustration of a foolish young man who succumbs to an adulterous woman; "he follows her as an ox goes to the slaughter...he does not know that it will cost him his life" (Proverbs 7:7-24 NASB).

All of us face temptations. Jesus was tempted in every way just like we are, yet without sin (Hebrews 4:15). God's Word tells us to "flee immorality," not keep placing ourselves in positions of temptation (1 Corinthians 6:18 NASB). If we have trouble on the home front, the answer is not to put in more hours at work nor focusing on our career rather than family. Instead, we must call a "time out" on everything else, seek godly counseling and rebuild our home.

Is an immoral "fling" or career advancement really worth the cost? As followers of Jesus, isn't our most important priority doing what is right in God's eyes?

†

I Don't Need a Marriage Conference

"I don't think we need to attend a marriage conference do you?" I asked. Hey, after all, I was a Christian man, treated my wife well, and knew the magic words, "You're right honey, I was wrong." For over twenty years I had truly proven to be the "perfect husband."

My loving wife pointed out that as wildland firefighters we attend safety refreshers every year. Wouldn't a marriage "refresher" be just as important? Catching her tone of voice, I began to re-think my objections. Sure, I thought, it couldn't hurt. Of course it didn't hurt. In fact, just as our fire refreshers help us refocus on the basics of fireline safety and keeping out of harm's way; the marriage refresher reminded my wife and I of some biblical basics to build and protect our marriage. Plus, it gave us a good excuse to have a weekend away in a nice setting.

In Ephesians 5:21 we are told to "submit to one another out of reverence for Christ." Initially, when my wife suggested we look into the marriage "refresher" I resisted. I had other plans for the weekend. I wondered if people would think we were having problems, etc. But I quickly learned that by going I was saying to my wife that our marriage was a priority and that I wanted to keep it strong. That's not a bad thing, is it?

†

My Dad Died

The phone rang early on Sunday morning. "Rick, this is Jim Barton," the voice said, "Dad died last night." What to say, how to feel? My parents had divorced when I was young and for over ten years I had not talked to Dad. He had remarried, had two sons and I hadn't even met them until last year. Now one of them was calling to tell me that my dad had died.

Had this happened during that ten-year period how would I have felt? I had never shared with my father about Jesus. I had never reached out to him and his wife and told them about what had happened in my life.

While in college I had given my life to Jesus, married a godly woman and started a ministry. As our children began to grow they began asking about my dad. "When are we going to meet him" they kept asking? It was becoming more and more difficult to reconcile my new life in Christ with the wall I had built towards my father. Finally, the time came when it was impossible. My dad wrote me a letter. "Please forgive me," he said.

As a follower of Jesus, I really didn't have a choice, did I? We were going through the area where my dad lived in a few weeks. I wrote him and said I'd like to see him and introduce my family. In two days the phone rang, "Rick, this is dad" the voice on the other end said. Caught off guard I said, "Who?" We met and began to build a relationship. I was able to share my testimony and how he could come to know Jesus. Eventually, we met his wife and sons and were able to share with each of them as well. His wife even asked us to write down the words to the "sinners prayer" so they could pray it together.

Three years ago, my dad entered an Alzheimer's unit. For the past year he didn't recognize me but his wife noticed he always became peaceful when I sang hymns and prayed with him. And now, I believe he's in heaven. And it all started because I had a wife and kids who held me accountable to my faith.

†

I Can't Do That

The Pastor looked at me with troubled eyes, "I can't do that!" he repeated. It was after the service had ended and everyone else had left.

"What do you mean I asked?" The pastor was obviously in anguish. "I can't do what you taught on tonight" he said. "When you said that Jesus tells us to forgive others or else He won't forgive us, it hit me. My brother used to abuse me when I was a child and I've always sworn that the next time I saw him it would be at his funeral. Today they called me and he's in the hospital and may not live. I can't go ..." his voice trailed off.

I had known this pastor for many years and he always seemed to have a cloud of despair hanging over him. He'd had family tragedies, financial struggles, and what seemed to be in many ways an unproductive ministry. Yet, he was a good brother and I cared for him a lot. Tonight, as I taught on the Lord's Prayer

(Matthew 6:9-13) the verses immediately following had impacted him. In Matthew 6:14-15 Jesus says, "For if you forgive others for their transgressions, your heavenly Father will also forgive you. But if you do not forgive others, then your Father will not forgive your transgressions" (NASB).

"Brother," I said, "I can't tell you what to do, but I'll take care of things here for the next few days if you like." The next morning he called as he was driving.

The following days were full of miracles. My friend arrived at the hospital and met his brother's wife. She told him that his brother had recently come to Jesus and would want to see him. Unfortunately, his brother was in a coma. When my friend went into the room and began to pray, his brother regained conscious-ness! They prayed together, gave and received forgiveness. Then the brother slipped back into the coma. Within a few days he passed into glory.

But, the miracle didn't end there. I didn't see my pastor friend for a year. When I passed his way again I found a new man. He had been set free! The Lord opened up a new ministry for him in the local jail. He was having an effective outreach with inmates and officers alike. His attitude at church had been transformed. His life had meaning and purpose again. Do you think the healing of his relationship with his brother had freed him to be a Spirit-filled witness? I wonder ...

†

A Waste of Time?

"Why are you wasting your time with that stuff?" an exasperated voice exclaimed over the phone.

I had just explained that I wouldn't be available for a wildland fire dispatch because I had accepted some preaching assignments. A busy fire season is underway, and for those of us who work as cooperators, this is the time to pay the bills. My friend immediate-ly apologized, but his reaction was somewhat normal. Why trade the income of 14-16-hour days for the small honorariums of a few country churches?

The answer has to be "priorities." I firmly believe that God (and my wife) gives me periodic priority checks. What has first call on my time, thoughts, and schedule? Jesus put it this way, "But seek first His kingdom and His righteousness, and all these things will be added to you," (Matthew 6:33 NASB).

Did I feel awkward and a little nervous when I turned down the assignments? You bet. Did the Lord bless during the church services and bring folks into His kingdom? Yes, again. Did He provide for every need, and even work in some fire assignments between the preaching? Of course!

Well, well he did it again. After returning last night from a fire in Utah, I made a commitment to take my family on a short trip. But before we left, we checked the college fund balance. Somehow, even though I've been out a lot less on fire assignments, the money needed for my son's fall tuition is in reach.

What do you know about that?

†

What Will Be On Your Tombstone?

"He was a liar, a cheat and a fraud."

What a way to be remembered! Recently, I read a list of tombstone epitaphs. This one, apparently written by a not-so-loving relative, really grieved my heart. But it also made me wonder. What would someone put on my tombstone? I know I'm headed to heaven because I've trusted Jesus; but what legacy will I leave behind to my family? What words will describe my life? What was my life devoted to? "He fought forest fires.?" "He never missed a day at work?"

Charles Spurgeon, famous preacher of the 1800s said, "A good character is the best tombstone...carve your name on hearts not on marble." Was former baseball player/evangelist Billy Sunday right when he said, "Live so that when the final summons comes, you will leave something more behind you than an epitaph on a tombstone or an obituary in a newspaper?"

So how do I do that? How can I make a "legacy" and not just a "living"? Maybe the first thing I need to do is to think about what really makes a difference.

One day in the Forest Service I expressed a frustration to a co-worker and threatened to resign. "Don't think that's going to bother them Rick," he said. "It'll be like a rock thrown in the water, there'll be a ripple for a moment then nothing. Stick around and you might be able to make a difference." That was wise counsel. And, even though I struggled to believe that my leaving would be so inconsequential, I realized he was right. Just doing my job wasn't building a lasting legacy.

Would financial success be the answer? As King Solomon discovered, wealth, sex, and pleasure were all worthless in the end (Ecclesiastes 2-3).

On a fire outside of Tahoe, CA, a man I hardly knew ran up and gave me a big hug. He began to tell me how I had influenced his life for Jesus. A woman in a fire class pulled me aside to tell me how I had "saved her life" by something I had said teaching a safety refresher. A Forest Service leader told me how I had convinced him to fight cancer and live by sharing the plan of salvation in a hotel lobby. I began to understand, a life focused on living for, and sharing Jesus would produce a legacy!

The Apostle Paul went through "hell and high water" to build a legacy. He did it by loving those who hated him, sharing the salvation of Jesus with anyone who would listen, and being both tough and tender as he nurtured new and old followers of the Savior. He cared, he loved! He had his priorities right.

Just before he was beheaded by the neurotic Emperor Nero, Paul could say, "I have fought the good fight, I have finished the course, I have kept the faith" (2 Timothy 4:7 NASB).

I'd like that on my tombstone, wouldn't you!

✝

Another False Alarm?

It was a real western Colorado winter and temperatures were dropping well below zero. Streets were icy and school was almost out for Christmas break. There had been a rash of false alarms at the college, all at night, and most were alcohol related.

The pagers went off again, suppers left to grow cold, kids watching mom or dad racing out to the car, and loved ones praying for a safe and speedy return. Once again, the call was to a college dorm. But this time, things were different. Smoke was pouring out of windows; students were hurrying out of their rooms, clutching a few belongings, coughing in the freezing air. This was the real thing.

As the well-trained volunteers struggled to break the ice away from the hydrants, clear paths for apparatus and string hose; others hurriedly tried to secure the building and ensure that all the students were evacuated.

Within an hour, things looked better. The flames were gone; ventilators were going full force and a semblance of calm settled in. Suddenly, the word spread. A body had been found. Somehow, in a floor already cleared, a student had returned. Some said for a stereo, others thought drugs. Nevertheless, he had slipped past police and perished inside. The sense of accomplishment was shattered. Despite their best efforts, a life had been lost.

Two lessons loomed large as the units stood down that night. One, no matter how often the alarms are false, the next one might be real. And two, stuff is just stuff. There's no possession worth giving your life for.

At least one person was reminded of Jesus' words, "What good is it someone to gain the whole world, and yet lose or forfeit their very self?" (Luke 9:25).

†

Confidence and Complacency

It was an 800-acre fire in Western Colorado. The first 24 hours had been crazy with the wind driving the flames toward numerous structures. I was called in as safety officer for the incident.

The wind had died down and our crews were making great progress on completing a line around the perimeter. I was confident we had a handle on the fire and that it was safe for me to escort local media to the line. So, outfitting them in Nomex, I piled them into my vehicle and off to the fire we went. After contacting the division supervisor, I lined out our guests and they began to shoot pictures and interview firefighters. Before long they wanted to go deeper into the burn area, and then further still. I became complacent.

Have you ever allowed confidence to become complacency? As followers of Jesus we are on a mission. The Lord made it very clear what our priorities are to be when He gave us these two commandments: love God with all our heart, soul, mind and strength; and love our neighbor as ourselves (Mark 12:30).

He has also given us a commission, to go and make disciples, followers of Jesus around our neighborhood, country and world (Matthew 28:18-20). Have we become so confident in our relationship with the Lord that we've become complacent?

As the media crews stretched further and further into the burned area, suddenly my friend the Division Supervisor showed up. "Barton, what are you doing with all these folks in here?" Embarrassed, I gathered up my chicks and moved them back to the rig, mindful not to let confidence lead to complacency.

†

A New LCES!

I was on a forest fire near Norwood, CO. As I circled the fire trying to ensure that our forces were being kept safe, I made a stop at our heli-base. There on a wall I saw a new definition of our tried and true, LCES.

As every wildland firefighter knows, LCES stands for Lookouts, Communications, Escape Routes, and Safety Zones. All should be in place before we engage a wildland fire. Doing so has saved many lives over the years. This four letter acronym was developed by the late Paul Gleason, a hotshot superintendent who knew that in the heat of battle, we sometimes forget the "Ten Standard Fire Orders," the "18 Situations that shout Watch Out" and the "Common Denominators." He boiled everything down into an easy to remember foursome, Lookouts, Communication, Escape Routes, and Safety Zones.

But on the wall at the heli-base there was a new LCES, "Locate Cooler, Establish Shade." Funny, yes, but is it really? As we look at the fatalities, serious injuries and near misses on incidents, isn't the main cause a lack of following our basic protocols? Do we get distracted from our mission and focus on our comfort?

How about in our daily Christian life? Most of us started off strong when we received Jesus as Savior and Lord. We knew we were in a battle for our eternal souls and those around us. We put on the "whole armor of God" (Ephesians 6:10-18). Our big four was found in Acts 2:42, we devoted ourselves continually to reading and studying the Bible, staying in fellowship, renewing our vows to God and each other in communion, and talking to God continually in prayer.

Have we forgotten what is most important—what our priorities should be? Have we slipped into a new big four? *Lazy Christians Elude Service*? Just wondering...

†

But Lord, They're All Mormons!

The call was to a fire in Utah. It was a "managed" fire that had potential but for the most part was behaving. How was the Lord going to open doors to share Jesus with my fellow firefighters this time? I had served fire details in Utah before and knew that many folks living there weren't Mormons. And, the ones who were, were often unaware of the fallacies of their leader's teaching. Most of the Mormon firefighters I had met were nice people and I genuinely cared for them.

As I arrived on the fire I was told I wouldn't stay at camp but rather at the Ranger Station. This would limit my one-on-one time with the crews so I prayed the Lord would still let me share. After all, as a Christian my first desire and highest priority is to serve Christ and be His witness in all I do.

The first Sunday, I traveled to where the crews were working. I had a Fellowship of Christian Firefighters (FCF) patch on my fire shirt and one of the men asked about it. When I mentioned that I sometimes held chapels and gave away firefighter New Testaments he asked for one. His friend looked at us and said, "I'm not very religious, but could I have one too?" The next day, one of our task force leaders approached me after the morning briefing. "Hey," he said, "One of the engine captains wants to see you. He wants to do what you're doing." It turns out that the captain had recently come to Christ and wanted to start an FCF chapter in Utah. After he and I shared, we prayed together. Later, as I passed his engine he flagged me down.

"The guys on my engine asked what we were doing. When I told them, they asked me to pray with them as well! And, they all want Bibles!"

The last day I was on the incident another blessing happened. My trainee noticed my *Answering the Call* New Testament and asked for one. This day we had an hour-long trip to the fire line. Rather than try to force the conversation I prayed silently. Before long he opened up and shared his disappointments with Mormonism. I was able to share the Gospel and encourage him to look beyond that teaching and turn instead to the Bible and to the Jesus who loves him so much. "Always be prepared to give an answer to everyone who asks you to give the reason for the hope that you have" (1 Peter 3:15).

✝

There's Got to Be More to Life Than This!

I was just going in for a cup of coffee between fire assignments. As I passed one of the restaurant's booths, I saw a local rancher who motioned me to sit down. After a couple of moments of small talk, he looked over and said, "There's got to be more to life than this! Sure, I was baptized as an infant, and then confirmed as a kid, but there's something missing." I admit, I was taken back. The rancher was wealthy, had businesses in two states, a good wife and kids, but something was missing.

After I regained my composure, (put my eyes back in their sockets), I was able to share the thing he was missing. He had been exposed to "religion," but had never entered into a "relationship" with Jesus Christ. Like many of us, he had put in time in church, served some, gave some, but through ignorance or neglect never personally confessed his sins to God, asked forgiveness on the basis of Jesus dying on the cross in his place, and yielded direction of his life to Christ to be his Lord. He hadn't been indwelled with the Holy Spirit. He had never been what Jesus called "born-again" (John 3:3), and that meant that he was on the outside of the abundant life, looking in.

I shared that message as best I could and he left, mulling it over in his mind.

How many of those around us, or even those reading these words, realize that there's more to life than they're experiencing?

Instead of trying to fill the void with worldly possessions, alcohol, drugs, or immorality, reorder your priorities and understand that there's only one solution that really works. Yes, the only way to really experience the fulfilling, meaningful life we were created for is to return to the Creator. To humble ourselves before God, ask forgiveness for our sin and rebellion against Him, trust Him to forgive us because Jesus died in our place and rose again, and turn our lives over to Him to be our Lord and Master. Then, each day ask Him to fill us afresh with His Holy Spirit. Make time each day to read some out of your New Testament, make time to attend a Bible study and worship at a good Bible teaching church, and start talking and listening to God all through each day.

God does love us and have a purpose and plan for our lives that will give us lives of significance and purpose. There really is, "more to life." Don't miss it!

†

The Christian Fire Triangle

The fire was starting to get away from initial attack forces on scene. A dormant spark in an abandoned campfire had caught a breath of air. Ridge-top winds fed it with oxygen and then pushed it into dry grass only a foot away. By the time someone spotted the flames it was already an acre in size and gearing up for a run through sage and grass into timber!

Every wildland firefighter knows that for a fire to ignite and spread it needs three essential ingredients; fuel, heat and oxygen. Without these, it goes out. We try to break this "Fire Triangle" by removing at least one element. We try to cut a fire line between the fire and fuel, cool the fire with water or smother it with dirt.

In Christ's body, the church, there seems to be the same dormancy as was in that abandoned campfire. Maybe in your life as well? There's potential but a lack of flames. New followers of Jesus seem to be on fire, but after awhile they too often seem to "cool" off. Yet we see some saints around us who never seem to lose their zeal, no matter how long they've served, or how many trials they've endured. What's their secret? How can we stir up the flames within us? (2 Timothy 1:6).

Perhaps it's like that smoldering campfire. We only need one or more elements in our Christian life to be restored in order to ignite! What would those elements be?

A forest fire needs a "heat" source to get started. An abandoned campfire, a lightning strike, or a dropped cigarette will suffice. Without heat there is no fire. You might say that the "heat source" in our lives is our salvation. A few years ago, a church researcher interviewed members of his evangelical denomination. He was concerned because few members were active in sharing their faith. He determined that nearly one-half of the members of churches he visited were unsaved, not born-again, eternally lost! You can't stir up what's not there!

I was one of that "heat-less" group growing up. I attended a good church weekly, served, led the music, looked and felt like I was a Christian. Thankfully, I encountered some followers of Jesus whose lives and words showed me the difference between "religion" and a "living relationship" with Jesus Christ. I confessed my sins to God, asked Him to forgive me on the basis that Jesus died on the cross to pay my "death penalty," and yielded my life to Him as my risen Lord. The fire was lit!

But that initial flame has to be fed. Once we've given our lives to Jesus, the "fuel" of God's word and the "oxygen" of the Holy Spirit are necessary for us to continue to grow in zeal and faith.

Everyone who's sat around a campfire knows that without a steady diet of wood, the fire goes down to embers. In our lives as Christians we need to feed on a constant diet of God's word, the Bible. Not necessarily trying to place the whole "log" in at once, but starting with a consistent reading of a chapter or two every morning; asking God to speak to us as we read. I get a lot of "reading" done driving to work, listening to Bible studies on CD. (And then, of course, obey what you read!)

The oxygen of the Holy Spirit is the third essential element in living an "ignited" life. Just as a fire without oxygen loses its power, a Christian life without the continual filling of the Holy Spirit becomes anemic. We just can't "huff and puff" enough on our own to keep the fire lit. When we receive Jesus as our Lord and Savior, the Holy Spirit comes into us (Acts 2:38, Romans 8: 9-10). But that's not enough. He wants to continually fill us, day after day (Ephesians 5:18). The Holy Spirit is probably the most ignored, neglected Person of the Trinity. Yet, He is the third essential part of the "God Triangle." We need to ask Him to fill us daily, to guide us and empower us to be consistently zealous for our Lord.

Do you really want to be a "smoldering saint"?

Wouldn't you rather be "on fire" for our Savior?

†

CHAPTER TWO

Prayer

Seeking God and the Holy Spirit

"Do not be anxious about anything, but in every situation, by prayer and petition, with thanksgiving, present your requests to God."

Philippians 4:6

Run the Flag Up and
Begin Each Day With Prayer

"Tell me about the shirt," the medical unit leader asked.

Two weeks ago, I was dispatched to the Beaver Fire in Western Colorado. Fifty mile an hour winds had pushed the fire up steep hillsides, engulfing several thousand acres. I had been on the fire for two days when the Type 2 Incident Management Team arrived. As a line safety officer, I was in direct contact with Casey, the medical unit leader. He approached me and asked about my Fellowship of Christian Firefighter (FCF) t-shirt. Turns out he's involved with a group of firefighters in Rapid City who have a Bible study and had been praying about aligning with other believers in the fire service.

While we were talking, Jon walked up. Jon's a paramedic from the Denver area, pretty young in the Lord. He joined the conversation and at end of shift we had a time of prayer. Later,

Lew from OR, Bill from KS, Steve, Paul, Vic and others identified themselves as brothers in Christ. In a large part this happened because of the FCF t-shirt.

Whenever I arrive in fire camp I intentionally wear an FCF shirt. I also wear one at checkout. Those are times I don't have my Nomex shirt on and when I have to visit the largest number of folks. Almost always when I wear the shirt, someone asks me about FCF and what we stand for. That gives me an opportunity to tell them about Jesus.

Years ago, I heard the expression, "Run the flag up the pole and see who salutes." What they were saying is, let those around you know that you are a follower of Jesus and see who responds. I find I don't have to be "in your face," although at times that may be appropriate, but generally if I just drop a word, ask a question, or wear a Christian firefighter shirt, those who have a spiritual interest respond. As a result, I have the privilege of praying with folks, giving out *Answering the Call* New Testaments, and sharing the great news of Jesus.

What's the bottom line? Just as we have certain fundamentals in wildland fire, such as anchor, flank and pinch, there are also certain fundamentals in sharing our faith. Every day I pray, "Lord, please fill me with the Holy Spirit, and lead me to folks I can share you with." Then I look for the doors to open! Of course, in addition to the "flag" we run up, we need to be living the best example we can be to encourage people to want to "salute."

Oh yea, on the way out of camp the Lord seemed to tell me to "slow down," there might be one more person He wanted me to talk with. I resisted for a moment, knowing if I hurried I'd get back just in time for a long-scheduled dentist appointment. But, I slowed down. And sure enough, one more man stopped me, asked a question about FCF and shared his testimony.

As it turned out, I did make my appointment after driving three hours and promptly fell asleep in the dentist chair.

†

But I Don't Go to McDonalds During the Week, Lord!

A strange thing happened this morning as I was driving to my usual restaurant for coffee and Bible study. Just as I was passing McDonalds I saw an out-of-town wildland fire engine parked in front. I felt an urging to go in but resisted it. "My" place to meet with the Lord was another block down the street. Still, the prodding in my spirit continued. "OK, Lord, I'll go back, but I sure hope this is you."

As I walked over to the engine crew I immediately recognized two old friends from previous fires. They introduced me to the "rookie," Ryan, a young man in his early twenties. Ryan noticed my Fellowship of Christian Firefighter (FCF) shirt and asked if I was a Christian. I responded "yes" and gave him an *Answering the Call* New Testament I always carry. At that moment, a Christian family from out of town grabbed me and we had a moment of great fellowship. And then, a backslidden brother asked where our church was meeting.

Finally, things settled down and I began to read the Word. Ryan reappeared and sat down with me. "I can't believe this," he said, "I was praying last night that God would show me how to be a witness on fires. I asked Him if anyone else was out on the fireline sharing Jesus. And you showed up."

I admit, I don't always listen for the still, quiet voice as I should. And, sometimes I even deliberately disregard its urgings. But today I listened and wow, what a blessing.

"Lord, fill me with your Holy Spirit, 24/7, that I may hear and obey."

†

You Stink

Recently the Wall Street Journal ran a feature article on a famous Christian athlete. The magazine writer sat in the stands with his young son listening to some "fans" hurling "f-bombs" at their own player through three quarters of the game. Then, in the final minutes, the young athlete made some phenomenal plays and against all odds won the game!

What would cause such viral treatment from even his own supposed fans? Why is this particular athlete both revered and reviled? Is it because as a second-year player he has shown inconsistency as he grows into his role? Maybe; but there seems to be something more here.

The athlete is a Christian. Not a tongue lashing, in your face, "turn or burn" believer, but one who whether he wins or loses expresses his trust and devotion to Jesus Christ. In a sports world tainted with drugs, immorality, and every other disgusting and degrading vice, he is a fresh and wholesome face. So why the attacks?

Perhaps it's a playing out of 2 Corinthians 2:14-17 which tells us that when we are filled with the Spirit of God we "smell" like Jesus. To those who are open to Him, we are a sweet-smelling fragrance of God's love. To those who are fighting God, our very presence and testimony brings conviction.

When I return from a forest fire assignment my wife generally meets me at the door with a hose and wire brush! My clothes smell like wood smoke, my vehicle smells like wood smoke, even my hair smells like wood smoke. I happen to love that smell because it reminds me of the hard work, camaraderie, and experiences on the fire! But if I've been working around a dump fire, sewer plant or burning tires, the stench repels me.

We smell like where we've been! If we're staying close to Jesus, reading the Bible, being active in fellowship, active in prayer, we'll "smell" like Jesus! If we're spending all our time in the sewers of this world, we'll stink! If we smell like Jesus, some folks will be drawn in, while others will become angry as their sin is exposed. How they respond isn't really what matters. What matters is staying so close to Jesus that we "smell" like Him.

†

The Eyes of Texas Are Upon You!

"Rick, the folks down there need help. They've had an 'incident within an incident' and some of the local staff are feeling over-whelmed."

Apparently, a firefighter from Oregon, was leading a dozer through thick brush in the dark when he tripped and the dozer ran over him. Now, he was clinging to life in a Dallas hospital. Texas and Oklahoma were experiencing historic fire activity with hundreds of homes and millions of acres burned. The local Public Information Officers were exhausted. They had taken only a few days off since Thanksgiving and this was February. Now, a terrible accident occurred bringing additional responsibilities.

The problem was, I had listed myself as unavailable, busy with my winter work and ministry. My plate seemed full. Even if I did go, it could only be for ten days, after that I had an important commitment. The reply came back; ten days would be fine, just come. It was a tough decision. I needed the Lord's direction. After prayer, and calls to my wife and work supervisor, I was on my way to Texas.

Initially, it seemed I'd made a mistake. I landed in a Dallas ice storm and had to spend a day in a motel waiting for the roads to clear. Rain and fog slowed the fire activity. Yet, as soon as I arrived at the Incident Command Post, I sensed that God was in this trip. The Information Officer turned out to be a Christian. We began to pray together for the injured firefighter and other needs on the incident. Soon, other members of the suppression effort came in for prayer as well. I gave away copies of the *Answering the Call* New Testament. The Incident Commander approved my request to hold a chapel service which went very well. In addition, a coworker began to ask questions about the chapel service. His questions opened the door to share Jesus.

When I left Texas, I lifted up a prayer of thanksgiving. I had accomplished my task of giving the local folks a breather, met and prayed with wonderful brothers and sisters in Christ, held a chapel service and shared Jesus with someone who hadn't met the Savior yet.

I was reminded of Proverbs 3:5-6, (NASB), "Trust in the Lord with all your heart and do not lean on your own understanding; in all your ways acknowledge Him, and He will make your paths straight."

†

And Then He Came Back

What an interesting role I was in! We were on a large fire in New Mexico and I had been appointed the job of escorting media from around the world to the fireline. I had folks from Korea, folks from around the United States and local camera crews. On one particular day I had a mixture of in-state media and national photojournalists.

At the end of the tour we said our goodbyes. Then one man turned his truck around, came back and rolled down the window. "Would you pray for me?" He asked. Of course, I did. It hit me hard as he drove away. Here was a nationally recognized reporter, flown in from out of state to cover an important story; but one who had a need for another brother to pray with him.

The Bible frequently tell us to be ready "in season and out of season" to do God's work (2 Timothy 4:2). Sometimes this means being ready to speak in a church or share our testimony on a moment's notice, but other times it simply means being available to pray "on the spot" with someone.

Now, I just have to remember to expect Him to answer...

†

Boss' Timing!

Wildfire season was winding down. I had been on fires in three states so far but hoped for at least one more major assignment. A call had come wanting a strike team leader but I was already committed to help with a special program at church. Finally, looking at the calendar, I realized I had one day to be available nationally and fulfill a fourteen-day assignment. It had been a slow season and I had only one day to be dispatched when guys were waiting weeks for a call.

Asking the Lord to guide my schedule, I called dispatch. "One day is all I have for a national call to come in." We all sort of laughed. "We'll see," they answered. A few hours later the phone rang! "You're the luckiest person I know," the dispatcher exclaimed. "You're going out."

Was I lucky? No! I just know Who directs my path. And, of course, the next two weeks were filled with opportunities to share Jesus! "But seek first His kingdom, and His righteousness, and all these things will be added to you" (Matthew 6:33 NASB).

†

"Purpose Driven" Shirts

I just returned from a fire in Western Colorado. Lightning ignited a 900-acre blaze in Pinon-Juniper and forced the evacuation of twenty homes. My phone and many others rang and after a short night we were on the road.

When I arrived for the morning briefing at the ranger station, I wore my Fellowship of Christian Firefighters shirt. And, as usual, it opened the door for a conversation. Later in the day, a firefighter asked what it meant and the sharing began.

When Jesus said, "Let your light shine" (Matthew 5:16), I know He meant your attitude, good works and testimony. But, I've found that as I walk into fire camp with a Christian shirt, and even wearing one as I go through de-mob at the end of the incident, it almost always opens a door to share the love and story of Jesus.

Will some folks be "offended"? I guess so. There are always those who think God should be kept in a very small box somewhere. But for the most part, if I do the best job I can and have the best attitude I can, the shirt, (or hat, helmet sticker or bumper sticker) becomes a means for someone to identify my work and attitude with my Savior. Or sometimes, like the engine captain at midnight on a fire in Oregon, provides an immediate identification for a fellow Christian who was longing to pray with someone.

Over the past few years there has been a lot of emphasis on being "purpose-driven." "Purpose-driven" lives, churches, even businesses. I think that's great. But how about a quick prayer each morning about what shirt you wear?

†

Not Now, Lord

"Hi, can I sit with you?" He asked. He was a fellow I'd met a couple of times before. He was on our Forest Service trail crew and had attended an Annual Fire Refresher class I taught. "Sure," I answered. To be honest, I just wanted to read the paper for a moment, grab a quick lunch and head back to work.

He began the usual light conversation and I admit I was only half-listening. Then it happened. "Where do you go to church?" was his question. My mind finally caught on, he was trying to start a conversation about the Lord and I was being courteously oblivious! Ahhhhh, what a dummy I am.

Cass was raised in a Mormon home but was now in his late twenties and searching. I was able to share with him and pass on an *Answering the Call* New Testament. Since then several Christians who work with him have encouraged him and brought him to a Bible study.

Every day I try to remember and pray, "Lord, please fill me with Your Holy Spirit and lead me to someone I can share Jesus with."

†

I'm Going to Be Real Honest With You

We were walking up a hill to the dining tent. The firefighter next to me began to open up and share her heart. She was a wonderful person but living in sin and I believe the Lord was revealing it to her. As we walked she shared and asked for prayer.

I was in the midst of a fourteen-day assignment on two of the largest fires in the continental United States. The Wallow Fire in AZ (538,000 acres) and the Las Conchas Fire near Los Alamos, NM (150,000 acres). The amazing thing was the number of folks who wanted to talk to me once they knew I was a Christian. I wear an FCF patch on my fire shirt as well as a helmet sticker; but I think even more important, I try to show the love of Jesus by deeds as well as words.

I was weary physically after a succession of fifteen plus hour days, but inside I was energized as I listened and prayed inwardly that the Holy Spirit would give me wisdom. Should I confront her sin, ignore her sin? The Lord led me to just listen (not my most natural reaction). I could tell that the Spirit Himself was convicting her that her behavior wasn't right. As she finished, I offered to pray with her that the Lord would give her wisdom and help for her need. With a tear in her eye she looked at me and said, "Thanks for listening."

As I walked away, I began to second guess myself. Shouldn't I have come out more forcefully about the sinful condition she was in? Then the Spirit reminded me of Jesus' encounters with two women; the woman at the well (John 4:6-29) and the woman caught in adultery (John 8:3-11). In both cases the awareness of their sin became apparent. In one case the woman became an instant evangelist and in the other Jesus showed His compassion by saving her life, telling her He didn't condemn her, and then admonishing her to "sin no more."

I believe there are times when the Holy Spirit tells us to be confrontational about sin, especially when the person is unashamedly promoting it. Yet, at other times, He tells us to be still and let Him convict of sin, righteousness and judgment (John 16:8); not endorsing or ignoring the sin but showing compassion realizing that "there but by the grace of God go I."

†

Just What Are You Throwing Away?

The first time I saw a fire shelter, it was in a trashcan!

The year was 1977. The Meadow Lake Fire was near the town of Rifle in Western Colorado. My twenty-person crew was leaving camp to hit the fire line when we were given orange fanny packs. "Here's your fire shelter," someone said. As we walked another hundred feet we saw a trashcan filled with unopened packets of what appeared to be aluminum foil tents. Firefighters were throwing out the shelters and using the fanny packs to carry lunches, saw gear, or other items.

"What's a fire shelter?" someone on my crew asked. I didn't know. In fact, no one around us knew what it was or how to use it.

Over the years, fire shelters have been credited with saving hundreds of lives. These heat resistant tents, carried on our line gear, are a last resort protection from temperatures that can easily exceed one thousand degrees. Every wildland firefighter has to annually review their use and practice deploying one. Yet, on that day in Colorado, we were simply given the shelter without instruction as to its value or use. As a result, it was simply a heavy nuisance, one to be discarded and replaced with a more practical item such as lunch.

In our lives of following Jesus, do we discard the wrong things? Do we tire of reading the Bible, going to church, pursuing a holy lifestyle? Often, we aren't told the importance of these essential elements of the Christian life, or how to effectively apply them. As a result, we toss them out and replace them with "feel good" theology and "sloppy Agape."

Once a firefighter understands how valuable the fire shelter can be in time of need, they never leave camp without it. Once a believer discovers how important it is to hear God's voice through prayerfully reading His Word, how essential church attendance is in building up ourselves and fellow believers, and once we discover the joy a lifestyle pleasing to God brings, we don't want to miss a day without it.

Let's remember the example set for us by the early believers in Acts 2:42 NABS). "They were continually devoting themselves to the apostles' teaching and to fellowship, to the breaking of bread and to prayer." Not as a ritual we will want to replace with a temporary "lunch"— but as a vital, living part of our daily life.

✝

Six Minutes Till Takeoff

The siren at Ft. Wainwright, Alaska's smokejumper base, sounded for several seconds. Six minutes later the jumpship left the ground winging its way to some new fire in Interior Alaska. "Jump 55 en route to Bettles with six souls on board," the radio crackled. An hour later the jumpers arrived over a fire which had been reported as one acre between two small Alaskan villages. Only when they arrived, the fire was 500 acres and climbing to an eventual 64,000 acres.

2004 was then Alaska's second worst fire season in recorded history. Over 4.8 million acres burned, the size of the state of New Jersey. I spent thirty-three days working in the Joint Information Center at Fort Wainwright during that Alaska Fire Siege. The Lord graciously blessed as I held chapel services for fellow firefighters between shifts, counseled workers and residents and passed out *Answering the Call* New Testaments.

But the six-minute smokejumper responses really made an impression on me. Their call could come anytime during their shift. They could be eating, repairing gear, working out or even cultivating their small garden. But when the siren call came, everything was dropped and within six minutes they were dressed in full jump gear and leaving the ground! How could they do this?

First, they were prepared. Every smokejumper had his or her gear packed and ready for dispatch. They were trained and prepared for this very moment.

Secondly, they were willing to drop everything and answer the call. This meant half-eaten meals, unfinished projects and disruption of their daily routine. They were ready to endure hardship to try and accomplish their goal of catching new fires while they were still small.

It hit me, isn't this an example of what Jesus calls every Christian to be. In Luke 12:35. He tells us to, "Be dressed ready for service and keep your lamps burning." As a firefighter, my gear bag is always near the door, ready for dispatch. Am I just as ready to respond to Jesus' call to visit a person in need or share a prayer with someone in distress? Am I willing to lay down my daily routine and join other "souls on board" in going where He sends me to fight the fires of Hell? Am I willing to endure hardship to accomplish my Master's goals? Am I ready for His final call, to meet Him face to face?

I pray that each day I will be ready for my Lord's six-minute takeoff.

†

It Was the Highlight of My Season!

I had just returned from sixteen 'fun-filled' days on a fire in Montana. Now, only two days later, I was arriving on the B & B Complex in Oregon.

I was assigned as a line safety officer and given the night shift. I don't like night shift! When the sun goes down, I go down. And yet, I trust that God chooses my assignments. As I made my way through the crews on the division, an engine foreman noticed my Fellowship of Christian Firefighters helmet sticker. "What's that?" She asked.

As I explained, she broke into a wide smile. "Finally, another Christian to share with!"

The next evening, she brought her crew over to meet me and each asked for copies of *Answering the Call*. "This is the closest I've been to being in church all season" she said. "Our engine's been out on assignments constantly."

After a week, I was reassigned to day shift and given a new division to cover. As I moved around the division I began to meet with various crews and their superintendents. I soon discovered that several of the "Hot Shots" were fellow believers. As we met on the line, we would talk safety and have a moment of prayer together. What wonderful times of encouragement!

In the middle of this past winter, I received an e-mail from one of the "Hot Shot" superintendents. "Rick," he said. "Our prayer times were the highlight of my season." That was a great reminder to me that just taking a moment to let our light shine, to encourage one another, to shoot up a prayer together, can have huge ramifications. The Bible tells us to "not forsake the assembling of ourselves together, as is the habit of some, but to encourage one another," and "to stimulate one another to love and good deeds" (Hebrews 10:24-25 NASB).

So, on my next assignment, either night or day shift, I pray that I will be looking for the opportunity to give and receive encouragement in Christ.

But, that's not the end of the story!

"Smoke" from last summer's fire season: I have received several e-mails this winter from firefighters I shared Jesus with last summer. A "Hot Shot" superintendent said that our prayer time on an OR fire was the highlight of his summer. A battalion chief from CA asked for twenty *Answering the Call* New Testaments to give away. And, a college student from WY wrote to tell how our chapel service and firefighter Bible we gave him strengthened him throughout the summer.

Death Strikes Swiftly

This weekend I conducted a memorial service for a twenty-three-year old man. He had just stepped out of his piece of snow maintenance equipment for a moment. Somehow, the brakes failed and he was crushed beneath the machine. Twenty-three years old. His whole life seemed to be before him and yet in one instance he was face to face with eternity.

As I stood in a crowded ski patrol building on top of Crested Butte Mountain, I looked out at seventy-five or so family, friends and ski area employees. Some were crying, some had already been drinking and were passing a bottle around, and for most it seemed almost a party. Yet, as I called for attention and began to read the 23rd Psalm, the raucous crowd calmed and total silence filled the room.

As I read of the hope we have in Christ, and prayed for the family and friends, I realized that for many young people in this room, this was the closest they had been to the reality of death. One moment they had been working and laughing with Chris, and the next moment he was gone.

After the short service, we began to weave our way down the mountain in a torchlight parade, holding highway flares. Some begin to cry out, "This is for you, Chris!" hoping somehow, he could hear and see them. When we reached the bottom, each went their own way, to either drown out their thoughts, or perhaps to contemplate their lives.

Over 20 men and women died last summer on wildland fires in the United States. Some in burnovers, others in helicopter crashes and engine rollovers. Did they realize that they would face eternity that day? Do we realize that we will as well? Is our relationship with Jesus secure? Have we made our own personal commitment to Him? Are we walking close to Him, today? How about our family, friends and co-workers? Do they know that we love and care for them? Do they know of our love for Jesus and our eternal assurance?

The Psalmist prays that God will teach us to number our days (Psalm 90:12). I wonder if we should pray that as well?

CHAPTER THREE

Armor of God

Preparing For Service

"Therefore, put on the full armor of God, so that when the day of evil comes, you may be able to stand your ground, and after you have done everything, to stand. Stand firm then, with the belt of truth buckled around your waist, with the breastplate of righteousness in place, and with your feet fitted with the readiness that comes from the gospel of peace. In addition to all this, take up the shield of faith, with which you can extinguish all the flaming arrows of the evil one. Take the helmet of salvation and the sword of the Spirit, which is the word of God."

Ephesians 6:13-17

I'd Love to Help, But ...

We were conducting a prescribed burn in Taylor Canyon when the call came. A tourist reported a lightning strike up Texas Creek. I was the closest person to a rig and so off I went.

When I arrived on scene I found a small fire burning and a large snag that needed to come down. Protocol prohibited me attacking the fire alone, especially with the snag involved, so I was relieved to hear that another firefighter was nearby and in route.

As Linda pulled up, I yelled a greeting and asked her to help me with the snag. She gave me a helpless look and replied, "I'd love to help, but I left the station this morning without my PPE," (personal protective equipment). Even though Linda had great training, loads of experience, and was needed, she couldn't help. Our rules strictly forbid attacking a fire without the proper protective clothing.

Sometimes I miss the opportunity to help out in God's kingdom because I leave home unprepared. I forget that at any moment I may be called to respond to a call for help.

Do I start the day with prayer? Am I filled with the Holy Spirit? Are my ears tuned to hear the Master's dispatch to a needy soul? Have I dressed myself in the whole armor of God?

†

Kill the Rescuer

"Be careful," I warned the new recovery teams headed into the aftermath of Hurricane Katrina. "It's been several months since these folks were displaced and some are getting really tired of being victims."

The "Kill the Rescuer" syndrome is a phenomenon we occasionally run into on large wildland fire incidents. When families are forced from their homes by the advancing flame front, they generally understand. But as day after day goes by, even week after week, and they still can't enter the fire area, they get frustrated. They often lash out at the very people who are helping them. The firefighter, sheriff's officer, even the Salvation Army food worker is a reminder of their frustration. The only real answer is to show these victims that we are making progress toward letting them return home.

In my life as Christ's ambassador, I sometimes run into the same thing. Folks displaced by sin or circumstance strike out at me, the church, or even God. Well meaning social service workers and Good Samaritans alike feel the brunt of their frustration. The good deeds seem at best unappreciated, and at worst resented. It seems the more is given, the worse the response.

Perhaps, these hurting folks don't want to be treated as victims any longer. Maybe they're ready for the great news of Jesus and His offer of restoration. Perhaps they are ready to have a helping hand equip and empower them to move into their new life. Job training, parenting skills, and financial counseling are all tools to help them move from being rescued to helping rescue others. As we move through the catastrophes of peoples' lives, let's pray that we will be God's ears, hearts, and hands.

On a wildland fire, people from all different backgrounds, races and regions of the country come together for the common goal of putting out the fire. It's that way in Christ's church; 1 Corinthians 12 and Ephesians 4 record how each Christian is uniquely gifted and necessary in the body of Christ. Just as the fire effort suffers when a crew doesn't show up on time or fails to do its job, so the work of the Kingdom of God suffers if each Christian doesn't fulfill his or her unique, God-given task.

†

Love of Possessions Leads to Death In Southern California!

While serving in the Southern California firestorms for the past few weeks, I experienced some wonderful highs as I watched survivors rejoice at the grace of God and heard story after story of miraculous escapes. I watched as communities near and far poured out comfort and aid to those in need. I watched the Christian community embrace the homeless and distressed. I also experienced sad moments as I drove past families huddled around a pile of ashes, all that remained of their homes, vehicles, toys and earthly belongings.

But, my most tragic memories concern the accounts of residents who traded their lives for their possessions. One fellow fireman shared with me about a couple that escaped the fire only to succumb to the lure of treasures lost. When they returned to retrieve them, they were entrapped by the fire and perished. A few days later, in a new fire camp, the word spread of a resident who tried to return to his home, only to be stopped by a police roadblock. He slipped into the woods and circumvented the roadblock but then failed to return to his family. The next day searchers combed the blackened hillsides calling his name, only to discover his body. Killed as he stumbled through the ashen forest.

In a very graphic way I saw the truth of Jesus' words, "What good is it for someone to gain the whole world, and yet lose or forfeit their very self?" (Luke 9:25) In these tragedies it was not only spiritual but physical loss.

Another woman perished in the flames when she didn't take the warning cries of her neighbors seriously enough. She thought she had plenty of time to pack her belongings, gather her animals, put her affairs in order and then escape. Her burned truck and charred body are sad testimony that she was wrong. When the watchman sounds the warning, we had best respond quickly. (Ezekiel 33) When Jesus calls to "come, follow Me" we must immediately obey. When God's Word warns us not to neglect the offer of salvation (2 Corinthians 6:1-2), we dare not put our decision for Christ off.

As I drove I-15 out of my last fire camp, as I surveyed the ruins of home after home, life after life, I asked myself some hard questions. "Just how important are earthly belongings to me? Do I heed God's 'roadblocks' or try to press around them? And most importantly, how urgently do I take God's instructions and warnings in my life?" Am I fully equipped with "The Armor of God," have I appropriated all of God's "Personal Protective Equipment" and tools for the battle?

†

We Don't Know Where You're Going, But …

It was late in the summer of 1987. I was spending my Saturday afternoon working at the church when my district ranger came by.

"Rick," he said, "Northern California is in severe drought, and a huge front with lightning is in the forecast. Pack your bags. We know you're going somewhere, we just don't know where."

Sure enough, that weekend over 1400 forest fires started in California and the Northwest. The "Siege of 87" had begun. Monday morning's instructions were clear. "Don't get over thirty minutes from the station. You're going somewhere, we just don't know where." Within an hour the call came. "Head to Grand Junction to meet the rest of the crew. You're going somewhere, we just don't know where." And on and on it went. It wasn't until we were in the air that the pilot announced that we were headed to Redding, CA. And thus, we began twenty-eight "fun-filled" days of intense firefighting.

As a follower of Jesus, sometimes it seems that way as well. We sense His moving in our lives. We know He's calling us to prepare. But where will we go? What will He have us do? Sometimes, we become frustrated before we finally see His plan unfold.

"Be dressed ready for service and keep your lamps burning," Jesus tells us in Luke 12:35. The opportunity for service may be in the next five minutes, and/or He may be preparing us for some duty in the future. Can we afford to become complacent, self-centered, or upset because we don't know His next step? Or, should we have the pack ready and be prepared for dispatch.

†

Carelessness Kills Firefighter

"An experienced firefighter was killed today on a small fire because he placed himself in a position where he had no possibility of escape. His expectant wife is now a widow and his children fatherless because of his carelessness. Apparently, this firefighter felt that his great training and experience exempted him from following the basic safety rules he had so many times taught to rookie firefighters. A memorial service to his carelessness will be held this Thursday evening at the high school gym and will be immediately followed by his friends and family trying to regroup their lives and grasp a dramatically different future. A 'stupidity scholarship fund' will be established in his name."

OK, when's the last time you read a news clipping like that? Well, actually, at least once a fire season – if you read between the lines. We keep killing ourselves by breaking our own rules. We don't scout out the fire before engaging. We don't wear the proper PPE. We don't ensure that escape routes and safety zones are adequate. Every time I prepare an annual wildland fire refresher course it hits me again. How can we be so stupid? How can we keep putting ourselves and others in obvious danger?

How about this article?

Carelessness Destroys Christian.

"An experienced Christian lost his reputation, family and dragged the name of his Lord through the mud today. Apparently, this Christian felt that his great training and experience exempted him from following the basic Bible directions he had taught to new believers. He began to harbor lust. He indulged in pornography. He spent time 'counseling' with women in private. A memorial service to his carelessness will be held in the pits of hell as his friends and family try to regroup and grasp a drastically different future. A 'stupidity scholarship' will be established in his name."

When I'm working a small incident, I sometimes catch myself "bending the rules." Then, I remember those who have died on insignificant fires. A falling snag, a flare-up, a rollover and suddenly a number of lives are forever impacted. In the same way I think about my daily life.

Am I "careless" about God's work and will in my life? Do I forget the basic rules of thought and behavior? Am I fully prepared with the "Armor of God"? For the sake of my family, my co-workers and most of all, my Lord, can I afford to be "careless"?

✝

Who Needs Training!

"It's the same old stuff. What a waste of time! The 'Standard Orders', the '18 Situations', 'Lookouts-Communication-Escape Routes-Safety Zones', and worst of all, climbing into a fire shelter. Who needs it?"

I shook my head in disbelief as I prepared to teach our annual Wildland Fire Refresher. How can any firefighter have that kind of response? Interestingly enough, it's usually the "occasional" crew members who express these sentiments. Those who fill in behind the regular fire folks. On the other hand, those who have the most experience seem the most willing to undergo the training. Why's that?

Is it because those of us who face "the Dragon" most realize its danger? Can it be that if we're not actively engaged in the fire effort, we grow careless? Do we become impervious to the fact that not paying attention for one moment can cost a life? Perhaps a false sense of "I don't need the basics" can work into the mind of any of us.

I once heard that Coach Vince Lombardi, of the world champion Green Bay Packers, would start each training camp by holding up an object and saying, "Gentlemen, this is a football." He then proceeded to reiterate the basics of football to the world champions! And, they listened and applied every word.

How about the basics in my spiritual life? When I read in Acts 2:42 (NASB) that the early disciples "continually devoted themselves to the apostles teaching (Bible study), fellowship, the breaking of bread (communion) and prayer," I have to ask myself how am I doing? Do I think that I've grown so mature that I don't need to apply myself to these basics? If so, have I become an "occasional" Christian who doesn't realize how real the "Dragon" is? That kind of carelessness can cost me my spiritual life!

In over fifty seasons of wildland firefighting, I've read and heard about hundreds of wildland fatalities. It seems that nine out of ten of these deaths have been related to neglecting the basics. We fail to post a lookout, establish a safety zone, maintain good communications, etc. In the same time period, I've seen and heard about hundreds of spiritual failures. I have to say that at least nine out of ten have been related to neglecting the basics of Christian discipline. As one counselor who deals with pastors involved in moral failure says, "I no longer ask if the pastor stopped having a daily quiet time, but when?"

Our work is dangerous. The "Dragon" we face is real. Let's encourage one another to continually review and train ourselves in God's basics.

✝

This Fire Is Contained. Oops!

The radio announcer was giving a rundown on several New Mexico fires. The fire I was headed to, the "Lookout Fire," was started by a poorly extinguished campfire. But, the fire getting all the attention was one that had been declared 'contained' only hours before it exploded out of control.

The fire managers had let their guard down, the crews had been released, and then, disaster!

What happened? Had a weather report been missed, or ignored? Had the ERC's (Energy Release Components) been underestimated? Why were those who had the most experience and training caught off guard?

At this time, it's too early to tell the exact cause of the fire's resurgence. But there are some interesting points to ponder aren't there? Points that apply to our lives?

One of the great blessings of the Christian life is our victory over sin's control. As the Apostle Paul said, "You have been set free from sin" (Romans 6:18a).

The problem can arise when we let our guard down concerning past sins. If Jesus has delivered us from alcohol abuse or pornography, we must be careful not to be complacent about their potential to come to life once again. If we have experienced God's grace in overcoming bitterness or anger, can we afford to underrate their residual strength and send our "crews" of self-discipline home?

No! As the entire verse reads, "You have been set free from sin <u>and</u> have become slaves to righteousness." The initial knocking down of the fire is not the end of the battle. We must continue "mop-up" for an extended period of time. On a wildland fire, we spend days and even weeks of patrolling the fire perimeter, knocking down any flare-ups, cold-trailing and looking for potential hot-spots. Can we afford to spend any less diligence with our personal fires? Can we allow complacency to lull us into danger?

Of course not! Let's seek the Lord daily. In prayer, in reading His Bible, in fellowship, giving and witnessing. Let's post a lookout over our hearts and souls, being careful to snuff out even the tiniest smoke of sin. Become a slave of righteousness so the "contained" sins of your past don't explode to life!

See ya on the "big one."

†

What's That Above You?

The fire had erupted from a burning underground coal seam. Before long, it had encircled the town of Glenwood Springs, Colorado, and hundreds of firefighters had been mobilized. Homes were lost and even the area around the tragic Storm King Mountain fire had re-burned.

I was assigned to the public information function to work with media. Since I am line-qualified, I was given the task of escorting "Good Morning America" to the fire perimeter to film and interview a hot shot crew. Working with the division supervisor, I located a crew and we were on our way.

As we approached one of the squads mopping up around a tree, I noticed something very disturbing. A broken tree top, what we call a "widow maker," was hanging right above them. The squad was so intent on moving from the base of one tree to the base of another that no one had looked up to assess any hazards. The firefighters had neglected one of our standard protocols;

"Look up-look down-look around." Not wanting to embarrass the hot shots, I pulled the squad boss aside and asked, "What's that above you?" He looked upward and gave a gasp.

Do we ever do that? Do we ever get so busy "doing life" that we don't pause to assess where we are and what hazards are around us? Do we neglect periodic check-ups with our spouse and children? Are we watching for warning signs about our relationship with them, and with the Lord? Are we prepared and fully adorned with the armor of God? Sometimes the Lord has to send someone by our "tree" to remind us to look up-look down-and look around.

"Be alert and of sober mind. Your enemy the devil prowls around like a roaring lion looking for someone to devour. Resist him, standing firm in the faith..." (1 Peter 5:8-9).

†

The Winds Are Coming

It was a classic case of a slow-moving wilderness fire gone bad. A fire that was being managed for resource benefit, consuming acres of dead and diseased trees, had erupted one afternoon and destroyed a popular resort and was encroaching on another. I had transferred in from another fire as safety officer. Our incident command post was located in the dining hall of the second resort where the previous *Safety* had developed an evacuation plan.

Like many large or complex incidents, we'd been assigned a meteorologist from the National Weather Service. He set up shop with his computers, satellite antennas, and pixie dust to begin cranking out weather updates and forecasts. At our noon Command and General Staff Meeting he announced that within an hour we would receive strong downdrafts which would greatly affect our fire behavior. What should we do?

Jesus told us that He would return to earth to bring about our deliverance, but also that He would expect us to be doing His will, prepared for His coming. (Luke 12:35-36). He told us some would think that since He hadn't returned yet, they could kick back, abuse their positions and be lazy. (Matthew 24:43-46) Looking around, do we see that today? Do we see churches, denominations and individual believers acting as if Jesus wasn't going to return? Are we acting that way ourselves? Our Lord warned that He would come unexpectedly, while folks are going about their business as usual, and then they will suddenly be caught up in judgment! (Luke 17:26-30).

On the fire that day, we decided to notify all the crews and rehearsed our move to safety. Sure enough within an hour the microburst hit! We rang the bell and ordered the fire crews into the safety zone. No one was hurt, the resort was saved and the meteorologist received a new bottle of pixie dust, compliments of the incident management team.

CHAPTER FOUR

Witnessing

Spreading the Word

"Then Jesus came to them and said, 'All authority in heaven and on earth has been given to me. Therefore go and make disciples of all nations, baptizing them in the name of the Father and of the Son and of the Holy Spirit, and teaching them to obey everything I have commanded you. And surely I am with you always, to the very end of the age.'"

Matthew 28: 18-20

What Number Are You?

We were standing on a fireline in Northern California. The Division Supervisor noticed my Fellowship of Christian Firefighter (FCFI) patch and began the conversation. We discussed God, Jesus and the Bible. He wondered if Jesus was really the only way to know God and a myriad of other sincere, searching questions. Soon, it was time to resume our duties. I asked if I could pray with him and he readily consented. Then he said, "You remind me of Fred, the Hot Shot Superintendent I met two years ago. He told me the same things. Do you know Fred?"

Of course, I know Fred. We've prayed together on several fires. The Division Supervisor and I called Fred that evening. Then I gave him a copy of *Answering the Call* with the encouragement to read some each day and let God begin to answer his questions.

As I thought about it later, I realized this is what the Apostle Paul was talking about in 1 Corinthians 3:5-9. One of us plants the seed of God's Word in someone's life. Another waters it, and yet another harvests. Then others begin the process of nurturing the new Christian.

Most folks don't accept Jesus the first time they hear the Gospel message. It may take four or five times before they make a commitment to the Savior. Our job is to be ready to share as He opens the door. We never know what number we are in that person's life.

†

Here We Go Again!

The latest news out of the southwest isn't good. Although New Mexico has received moisture, much of Arizona is facing another tough, drought-plagued fire season. "Pack your bags, Rick, you'll be coming our way soon!" my former district ranger emailed. "The 2007 season looks to be a hot one."

Ok, so I'm a forest firefighting junkie. My adrenaline starts flowing in March and doesn't subside until November. But, sometimes it seems like a lost cause. We never seem to do enough prescribed burns. There's never enough mitigation around homes and communities. We always lose structures. And tragically, no matter how hard we train and emphasize safety, we lose men and women. Last year, twenty-four lives were lost battling wildland fires.

Sometimes I get the same feeling about trying to reach souls for Christ. For every man, woman and child that receives the Savior, a hundred seem to slip into hell. Am I, are we the church, really making a difference?

Then I remember the story of the little boy walking along the seashore. Before him lay hundreds of starfish that had washed ashore. He carefully reached down and threw one after another back into the sea. A man standing by remarked, "It's no use son, there are too many. You'll never make a difference." Without missing a beat, the boy replied, "I will to this one." We are making a difference. Every life we touch for the Savior, every soul redeemed from hell's clutches, matters.

"Therefore go and make disciples of all nations, baptizing them in the name of the Father and of the Son and of the Holy Spirit, and teaching them to obey everything I have commanded you" (Matthew 28:19-20a).

†

Don't Push Your Religion!

"Don't push your religion." That's what someone wrote on the comment card of an Annual Fire Safety Refresher I taught last spring. Not only did they make the comment, they hid the, *Answering the Call,* New Testaments I had placed near the free coffee, donuts and other fire giveaway's I provide for my classes.

My heart sank. The response to the class had been overwhelmingly positive. The mixture of Forest Service, Park Service and Bureau of Land Management firefighters had really jumped into the discussion and case studies I had presented. Every other response card had great remarks. But someone, anonymously, had been offended that I had placed the New Testaments out for anyone who was interested. I hadn't mentioned the Bibles or made comments about the Lord during the class, but this individual was upset. In my thirty summers of working in the Forest Service I had occasionally come across such animosity toward the Lord but nothing recently. I had several more classes to teach as we prepared for the wildfire season, what should I do?

The Bible warns us that there will be those who dislike us because we bring Jesus with us everywhere we go. His Holy Spirit indwells us and when we walk into a room they sense His presence. To those who are looking for God's love and forgiveness, they sense it in us and are attracted. To those who choose to rebel against God, we are like the smell of death, and they hate us (2 Corinthians 2:14-16). After my initial disappointment, and an assessment of whether I had "pushed my religion" or not, I decided to continue on as before. The constitution prohibits discrimination against people of faith. If I am only making New Testaments available to those who are interested, not pushing or coercing anyone, then it's my right. I began to pray for the person whose heart is in turmoil about the Savior who loves them so much.

Was I tempted to stop offering the Bibles? No! God has called me to share His Word, and share I will.

I just finished teaching this year's Refresher class to the same individuals. The small stack of *Answering the Call* New Testaments was in its customary place, near the free coffee and donuts. This time they weren't disturbed. Some were taken.

†

I've Started to Get Interested In God Again

"Don't let them send you to Texas, Rick. They have everything that bites, pokes and stings on that assignment!"

These were the encouraging words I received from a co-worker when I was dispatched to East Texas in April 2003. The Resource Order said that I was going as a Strike Team Leader to serve in the Columbia Space Shuttle recovery project. You've got to understand, I'm not nearly as rattled by a crown fire as I am by a rattler, copperhead, or cottonmouth. But off I went.

This was the beginning of one of the most exciting ministry times I've ever had on an incident. But it was not one without challenges. After sitting in the airport for five hours to catch our one flight to Denver, the flight was cancelled. So, a four-hour drive through a snowstorm was followed by an early flight out the next morning. As I entered the Incident Command Post and checked in, the Lord began to open doors for ministry. I started to talk with the check-in recorder. Turned out he was a believer and wanted one of the *Answering the Call* New Testaments. Then I had a "chance" meeting with the Incident Commander. I asked permission to hold a chapel for the crews on Sunday after shift. "No problem," he said. Things were going great. I met my Division Supervisor who turned out to be a great brother from southern California. Then I tied in with my two crews from the west coast and left for the field.

The enemy began to fight back. The Devil doesn't sit idly by when we start to work for the Lord. At the last minute, the IC withdrew his support for the service. Apparently, someone had complained that it wouldn't be interpreted into Spanish, that it might not be inter-denominational enough, etc. I was taken back. I had already begun to spread the word about the service. I could get angry or get praying. Fortunately, I chose the latter. Within minutes one of the overhead team reports that firefighters are asking about a service and that the IC had changed his mind. "Would I be available after all to do the service?"

Another enemy came up as I entered the briefing tent to prepare for the service–fear of failure. The area I was to use was filled with folks watching the NBA playoffs on a big screen TV. I was told that the television would be turned off and that I was to be given the briefing microphone to speak. "Oh great," I thought, "I'll make all these guys mad and probably only five or six firefighters will show up for the service." I offered to move the service to a small area at the back. "Oh no," my guide responded, "They all understand that you'll have the area for thirty minutes."

At the appointed time the TV was turned off and I strode to the microphone. Surprisingly, only a few left and others were coming in! As I welcomed the group and we began to sing, even more filtered in. Over twenty-five firefighters of all races and backgrounds joined in. And, just as great, another fifteen or so "hung out" at the edges of the tent watching and listening in. This second group is something that happens at every service I hold. Those who are curious are drawn to the perimeter. And because I had been given a mic, they heard every word. At the end of the service, I prayed with attendees, gave away all the *Answering the*

Call New Testaments I had (I thought), and even took the names and addresses of several more who wanted Bibles.

The rest of the assignment was interesting. Twelve to fourteen-hour days, beating through thick brush, jumping over copperhead snakes (I discovered that white men can jump, with proper motivation) and finding shuttle pieces. Every day someone came up to me and asked about the Lord – a young pastor's son on a fire crew, a member of overhead asking for prayer, someone wanting a Bible... As I mentioned earlier, I thought I had given away all my firefighter New Testaments. But, as I was packing to go home I found two more. Heading to the mess tent for my last meal in camp, another firefighter stopped me and asked for a Bible. I gave him one of my last two and sat down to eat. Another man sat down beside me. "Rick?" He said, "One of the overhead folks who left the fire, called back and asked for your name and phone number. She wants to find out where to get more of the *Answering the Call* New Testaments. She thinks her Sunday school class will buy a supply for her to hand out on incidents. And then he said, 'Can I get one too? I've started to get interested in God again'."

Yes, I was bitten and poked, but was I ever blessed.

†

Did I Forget the "One Thing?"

I was on a fire assignment in Phoenix when the man I was filling in for said, "There's one thing you really need to do..."

Ever hear that comment as your supervisor or predecessor leaves you in charge? I have, and then become distracted and totally forgot the *one thing* that was entrusted to me!

On that assignment in AZ, I was asked to handle media and public inquiries about any ongoing fires, but if there were none, the *one thing* I had to be sure to do was build line gear packs for media. The fire activity was slow, but my vehicle had issues, my feet had issues and I worked on other projects but never did the *one thing* I had been asked to do. What a dummy I am!

I just returned from a fire assignment in the south. As my predecessor left he said, "If you get time, there's *one thing* you could do that would really help." When my tour was over, I looked back and wondered? Did I do the *one thing*?

When Jesus left this earth, He told us there was *one thing* we as Christians needed to do. He told us to go into all the world and help people become His disciples; then to baptize them in the name of the Father, Son and Holy Spirit and to teach them to observe all that He commanded us (Matthew 28:19-20).

At the end of my assignment here on earth, as my Lord and I look back on my job performance, will I have remembered the *one thing*?

†

Those Books

"Do you remember those books you sent me last year?" the fire chief asked. Of course I did. I had served on a fire assignment in Western Colorado and this chief was the Incident Commander. At the end of the incident I gave him an *Answering the Call* New Testament and asked him to look it over and pass it around to the folks in his department. "If the guys would like some more, just call me," I said.

Two weeks later he did call. He asked for a case of "those books." Within days a box of New Testaments was on its way. After that I hadn't seen or heard from the chief.

Later, I was planning to speak in a church in his community I called and told him I wanted to honor and pray over the members of the fire, EMS and police departments during the meetings. In addition, I wanted to present the department with one of the "Flag of Honor" American flags which contains the names of the victims of 9/11. The chief agreed to pass the word around and then told me what was happening with "those books."

After the department received the case of *Answering the Call* New Testaments, he put them out in the station for men and women to pick up. Soon, most of the department had a copy. Since the building is used for other training, the chief noticed that other groups of emergency responders were taking copies as well! "We're kind of working our way through them," he said.

Lessons Learned? First, we don't ever have to be reluctant about passing out God's Word. It's especially easy when it's giving a fellow firefighter an *Answering the Call*. Second, we don't always know the long-term impact that one New Testament will have.

As Jesus said, "The harvest is plentiful, but the workers are few" (Luke 10:2). I think He means the problem isn't so much the unbelievers responding, it's getting the believers to step out and share.

†

Tebow Time

"Tebow, Tebow, Tebow, that's all I heard around here. If I hear him talk one more time about Jesus I'll ... I mean I believe in God and all but..."

Here in Colorado we heard a lot about this young Broncos quarterback named Tim Tebow. A man whose mother was told to abort him in order to save her own life, a man who surprised all the "talking heads" on the sports shows by leading the Denver Broncos to the National Football League playoffs. He's been on the cover of magazines, featured in the Wall Street Journal, and he'd dominated the sports shows for weeks.

But what caused this frenzy of interest, both positive and negative? Why were Marine Corps Honor Guards and fans across the country "Tebowing" (kneeling in imitation of the twenty-four-year-old player at prayer?) Perhaps it was a combination of his extraordinary platform as a "come from behind" winning NFL quarterback; and his open faith and testimony that every gift and ability He has is from the Lord Jesus Christ.

Does God really care who wins a football game? "Yes" and "No!" No, God isn't a Bronco's fan (even though sunsets are orange...). There are followers of Jesus on most sports teams. On the other hand, He does care intimately about everything that concerns us, our character and our witness for Him. Does Tim Tebow's public witness for Jesus mean God will make his passes better? His runs longer? Not necessarily, but it does mean that Tebow has used the platform God has given him to proclaim the name and message of the Lord Jesus Christ. This isn't a new thing; he has been faithful in the small opportunities throughout high school and college and now God has chosen to entrust to him larger venues (Matthew 25:23).

So the question arises, what have you and I done with the platform God has given us? Surely you realize that as firefighters and EMS personnel we are admired and respected by almost everyone, especially children. Are we using the position God has placed us in to bring Jesus into our circle of influence? Do we offer a prayer when there are needs around us? Do we carry a New Testament in our gear and read it during breaks? Are we active attendees and servers in a local church?

You may not think that you can make a difference, but you're mistaken! Here's a suggestion, each morning ask God to fill you afresh with His Holy Spirit and give you opportunities to shine a light for Jesus. Then sneak a look behind you and see who's "Tebowing" behind you!

†

Seedy Characters Caught Changing the World

"Can God really save my friend?" "What can I do, he's dying?" All of us go through times of wondering, or feeling inadequate when it comes to sharing our faith. It seems easier to just enjoy our Christian life and hope that God sends "someone else" to help those around us who are lost in sin. This is the story of two folks who didn't cop out.

This is about Deb and Ralph, two "seedy characters" that overcame those doubts and changed the face of eternity by an act of faith and obedience. This couple picked up a motorcycle New Testament (*Hope for the Highway*), available from Biblica formerly the International Bible Society. They prayerfully took it to their friend, a motorcyclist, who was dying. They lay it next to his bed and prayed for him. The man began to read the stories, and then the great news of the Gospel. In the days before his death he yielded his life to the Savior! As he slipped from this world into the arms of His heavenly Father, he asked them to sing the "Old Rugged Cross" at his bedside.

Imagine the joy of these "seedy characters" as they saw the results of sharing the "seed" of God's Word with this man! They realized what Luke meant when he told us that Jesus sent out the disciples "two by two ahead of Him to every town and place where He was about to go." (Luke 10:1). Jesus has given us the "seed" of the word of God and salvation. Our assignment is to go to those He leads us to and share it with them. These are places and people He is preparing to come to! As Luke goes on to say, "The harvest is plentiful, but the workers are few." Can He count on us? Jesus is looking for a few "seedy characters"!

†

The Case of the Two Seeds

Seed #1

My phone rang. It was a forest service fire manager from Oregon. We had worked together recently on a wilderness fire in California. I had come away disappointed. It was one of the few times I'd held a chapel service and no one had come.

The helicopter had dropped us off in a spike camp for ten days. There were twenty-five of us and when Sunday arrived, I invited everyone to come over to a log for church. No one came. Ouch! The same old struggle internally, could God turn my disappointment into His-appointment?

Later that day I gave an *Answering the Call* firefighter Bible to one of the men. He glanced it over, expressed his thanks, and nothing more was said. I prayed it would be a seed God could use, (Luke 8:11).

That night he called. He had begun reading the stories, and then the New Testament. God had touched him. Now he wants more to give away. He and his wife are starting to attend a local church and you can just hear in his voice that God is working.

Seed #2

My latest wildland fire was in CO, only a couple of hours from my home. There had been several homes lost and I had gone over to assist the local Public Information Officer. As I left the fire that evening I gave the Incident Commander/volunteer fire chief a copy of *Answering the Call*. He looked somewhat surprised and said "thanks." A few days later he contacted me. "Where can I get a case of those books?" He had already given his copy away to one of his men in the hospital. Now he wanted more to share with the entire department.

Just the little act of prayerfully planting a seed; giving away a New Testament, inviting someone to church or Bible Study, offering to pray with them over a concern, can be the start of something that will change that person's life for eternity! It just takes us being willing to step out. Each day I ask Jesus to fill me with His Holy Spirit, lead me to people I can plant seeds with, and to give me the courage to do so.

Bonus seed!

While I was in Oklahoma City, I gave a motorcycle New Testament *Hope for the Highway* to a lady who attended our meeting. She emailed me and it seems her family owns a motorcycle shop and ...

Are You the Guy With the Bibles?

I was at Ground Zero. The Pile was becoming The Pit. Even after several months, the remains of victims were being located, tagged and removed. Each time a body part was discovered, a recovery team was dispatched. My job was to give support to those teams. Working alongside a couple dozen Christians from around the country we fed, counseled and shared God's love with the 150 men and women working in shifts around the clock.

I had brought several cases of *Firefighter New Testaments* (the edition before *Answering the Call*) with me. Placing them on each of the tables I prayed that the Lord would use them to bring

light and encouragement to these folks. By the end of the week, almost all the Bibles were gone.

Suddenly, something happened that caught me off guard. A city fire chief approached me. "Are you the guy with the Bibles?" he asked. When I said, "Yes," he asked, "Could you get me 500 more?" That's right, 500. "Of course," I gulped. "Just let me know where to send them. I called the Fellowship of Christian Firefighters (FCF) office in Colorado. Yes, they could get the Bibles, and yes, they would send them. I called a Christian businessman who offered to underwrite the cost. Fortunately, the FCF leaders at that time could get them quickly, and within two weeks they were in the hands of the Fire Department of New York. And you know what God can do when we place His Word into the hands of firemen.

Here's the bottom line. We were able to distribute 500 *Firefighter New Testaments* because the supply was in hand.

†

Weddings, Lies, and Other Near-Death Experiences on the Fire Line

"I have to go home early, I'm getting married!" one person told me. "My husband was just sent on a fire and the people watching our kids are leaving town; I have to go back," said another. What's a crew boss to do? None of us had expected this fire assignment to stretch out for several weeks. We were sure we'd be home at the end of fourteen days. But the fires were so numerous and so extreme that the Secretary of Agriculture had extended all Forest Service fire crews indefinitely. We'd have one day off in a nearby town and head back to the line. To make things worse, we were making "Klamath death marches" daily on steep terrain and a heavy inversion was keeping us in the smoke constantly.

As I listened to the two crew members relate why they had to leave, I felt sympathy. After all, who could justify making the one miss their own wedding and the other worry sick about her children?

After arranging for them to fly home and ordering replacements, I discovered the rest of the story. The wedding wasn't for several months; and although the second lady's husband was on a fire, their children were being cared for by family members. Apparently these two folks had discovered that the commitment of serving on a fire crew was more than they had bargained for.

What about you; what about me? When we first heard the Gospel message it sounded exciting. Lay aside your old, self-centered life which was headed to nowhere but hell, and take up your cross daily and follow Jesus! (Luke 9:23). But what happens during those times when it's not exciting, when trials and tribulations come instead of joys and blessings? Do we abandon our crew, our fellow Christians, and go back to our old, "comfortable" life?

God's Word tells us that there will be tough times as we walk with the Lord on this earth (John 16:33); and yes, there will be times when we feel like giving up. But those who "finish strong" will receive the blessing! As the Apostle Paul said shortly before being beheaded by the Roman Emperor Nero, "I have fought the good fight, I have finished the race, I have kept the faith. Now there is in store for me the crown of righteousness, which the Lord, the righteous judge, will award to me on that day-and not only to me, but to all who have longed for His appearing." (2 Timothy 4:7-8)

By the time we finished that twenty-eight-day assignment, over half of our crew had to be sent home due to sickness from the smoke. But each one went home a respected crewmember. They finished strong.

"Lord Jesus, please help me 'finish strong'. Help me not abandon You or my fellow believers when the going gets rough."

✝

The Forgotten Bible

"I'll leave you a Firefighter Bible at the front desk," I promised my co-worker. He'd attended a fire class I taught and had approached me later, asking about the Lord. The next day I left the *Answering the Call* at the desk and prayed that God would use it.

The problem was he kept forgetting to pick it up. And, since our work schedules seldom overlapped, I couldn't remind him that it was waiting. Over a week went by and it still sat on the front desk counter. Finally, I apologized to the woman at the desk for it sitting there so long. "It's OK," she said, "I've been reading all the stories. I really like it." Once again, what I took as a "disappointment" turned out to be "His-appointment."

The end of the story? The fellow finally picked up the Bible, the desk clerk wants one of her own, and the Lord used the "forgotten Bible" to touch another life.

✝

In Season and Out of Season

I was finishing some work at Southern Seminary when the phone rang. "Are you available to go to Texas on a fire assignment?" the voice asked. "Not until next week," I responded, "I'm finishing up some work here and really can't leave. Sorry!" And that was the end of it ... or so I thought.

The 2011 fire season had been a busy one. I had been dispatched to Arizona, New Mexico (twice), and even Wyoming. Things had been winding down so I planned to work a couple weeks at the seminary and then get ready for my winter job teaching skiing. Somehow, I'd missed all the Texas fires this time.

I finished my work at the school, caught a flight back to Denver and was enjoying my drive home when the phone rang again. "Are you home yet," the same caller asked? And soon I was on my way to Houston and then Northeast Texas for two weeks. (Yes, Texas friends, I'm the one who brought the heavy rain to Houston in early October).

To be honest, I wasn't really excited to be going. I'd been on the road over twelve weeks on fires and ministry trips and wanted to be home. Still, I try to commit my schedule to the Lord Jesus and when dispatch calls, I trust it's Him sending me to someone to share with. Sure enough, my second shift of the assignment brought a co-worker into my life who was a great guy, just not a believer ... yet.

As I shared with him, he commented that his daughter and son-in-law were Christian firefighters and might want to talk to me. I knew this was another "divine appointment." As I talked to his daughter, I learned that she and her husband read the *Encourager* and gave out *Answering the Call* New Testaments. They had been praying that someone else in the fire service would share with her dad, and guess who God sent?

No, he didn't give his life to Jesus while I was with him, but I trust I was one of the "seed planters" God will use to help him come into eternal life (See 1 Corinthians 3:6-8).

Over the next two weeks I was able to give away as many *Answering the Call* New Testaments and *Stories of Faith and Courage from Firefighter and First Responders* devotional books as I could stuff in my gear bag; as well as share with other co-workers about Jesus. One safety officer waited till everyone left after morning briefing and began to ask me questions about God and the Bible. Once again, even though I thought the "season" was over, in God's timing it was still going strong! (2 Timothy 4:2).

What about you? Do you sometimes feel your "season" is over, on an assignment, at your job, or even in life? It's not, my friend. As someone put it, "Your purpose in life isn't finished until God calls you home." So, strap on your PPE, lace up those boots and join your crew; God's dispatch is calling us! The season's still going strong!

†

"Give Me a Scrench"

You're on a wildland fire in Montana when you throw the chain on your chainsaw. You need to take the cover off, start reworking the chain, and the fire is moving fast. You yell over your shoulder for your swamper to bring you a scrench. He looks at you and says, "A what?" Precious time and line is lost while you grab the saw kit and search for the tool.

You've arrived at a structure fire, people may still be trapped in the building and you need to set up quickly. You shout, "Grab a four-inch line and attach it to the hydrant. Then grab an inch and three-quarter cross lay and stretch it around the west end. I need water <u>Now</u>!" You turn to your helper and see the infamous "deer in the headlights look"; you know it's going to be a long night. And worse, someone may die because you can't get water to the fire quickly.

To the firefighter who's spent the time and effort needed to study the manuals, attend the classes and go through hours of hands-on training, things move pretty smoothly even when they're thrown into an emergency setting. But pity the crew that has a member who didn't think training was that essential, who had "more important" things to do, who thought that "someone else" would take care of the job.

Training in the fire service is crucial. Without it, we lose homes and even lives. Yet even more tragic are the eternal losses that follow poorly trained servants of our God and King! As one of the most listened to preachers of recent history, the gravel-voiced J. Vernon McGee said, "In my opinion, the greatest sin in the church of Jesus Christ...is ignorance of the Word of God. Many times, I have heard a church officer say, *'Well, I don't know much about the Bible, but...'* and then give his opinion, which often contradicts the Word of God! Why doesn't he know much about the Bible? These things were written afore time for our learning. God wants *you to know* His Word" (emphasis mine).

As followers of Jesus, we're the only Bible some people will ever read. They look to us to know what God says about something. And, as the world promotes such things as homosexual behavior and abortion, they expect you and me as Christians to speak God's truth. Even if they don't like what we say, they know they've heard the truth. As McGee said, if we just give them our opinion, we may very well be leading them away from God's truth and into Satan's snares.

"But," someone says, "I'm a fireman, not a preacher." True, we're not all called to stand behind a pulpit or venture into the deepest jungles; but we are called to study God's word, the Bible (2 Timothy 2:15). That way we can give God's answers. Answers that are always true. Answers that will lead folks to eternal life in Christ! Otherwise, we may give them well-intentioned, pleasant-tasting, poison which will eventually kill them spiritually!

Giving wrong feedback is as dangerous as confusing the mixture rate of diesel to gas for your drip torch. On a hot, dry day a good mixture is 70% diesel to 30% gas. Get that backwards and you better have your running boots on!

So how do I get it right? Three S's might help. First, <u>*Stop*</u> talking about something if you don't know what the Bible says about it. Tell the person you need to do some homework.

Second, *Study*. If you need help, ask your pastor or church leader for guidance in finding verses that deal with the subject. Then, be pro-active. Just like training is a continual process in our fire jobs, so it is in our Christian life! Get involved in a Bible study as well as start reading a chapter or two a day on your own. That way, when that unexpected question arises, you're already prepared. Third, *Share*. Sometimes that's the most difficult "S." A lot of us know what God says about immorality, gossip or lying, but the fear of what others may think holds us back. At that point we have to pray, dig deep inside for courage and trust the Holy Spirit to work! He promises His Word will always do His work (Isaiah 55:10-11)! After all, there's only one person we really need to please! The One who has given everything to and for us! Don't be a helpless helper, don't remain a Bible rookie, get into God's Book and train, train, train!

†

I Guess I'm Here to Get Away

"If dispatch doesn't call in the next four minutes, I guess I'm not supposed to go." Those were the words I told my wife as we sat in the living room. My ministry commitments had been heavy during fire season and I hadn't been able to find the 16-day opening needed to accept a national wildland fire assignment. To top it off, when I did find an opening, I hadn't received a call. I only had a two day "window" to be dispatched and no call had come.

Normally during fire season, I'm dispatched within a couple of hours of becoming available. In fact, I typically get calls even when I'm not on the available roster. But this time, silence. The one call I did get was to conduct a wedding the following day for a couple I didn't know. I asked the third party calling for a half-hour to pray before committing. Twenty-six minutes had passed and it looked grim for a dispatch. Perhaps the Lord was saying "Stay, and do the wedding." I was prepared to accept that, even though I would be disappointed.

Then, the phone rang. It was dispatch. "You're headed to Oregon." I turned to my wife and said, "Now, what would make this perfect is that the couple will have found a pastor." I called the number I had been given and told the man answering that I heard they needed a pastor. He apologized and said they had just obtained one. That began 15 days of one of the most Spirit-led assignments I ever had!

One of the things I've been learning as I walk with Jesus is that He wants to direct our steps, not just in general terms, but specifically. Yet, so many times we as followers of Jesus don't seek His specific will, purpose and direction. Instead, we do what seems good to us, leaning on our own understanding rather that committing our ways to Him and letting Him direct us (Proverbs 3:5-6).

My first stop was at the dispatch center to pick up my travel orders. Since it was late, I called and suggested they simply leave a packet on the door. Instead, the dispatcher, a brother in Christ, waited for me. He had encountered a serious marriage problem and we talked and prayed (off the clock) for an hour. The next day I arrived at a 52,000 acre fire near Burns, OR. The problem was, it was a grass fire and had gone out as quickly as it started. They were literally taking down the tents. Still, my Fellowship of Christian Firefighters patch attracted the attention of the Incident Commander and Information Officer. I was able to pray with them and give each an Answering the Call New Testament and *Stories of Faith and Courage from Firefighters & First Responders* devotional by Gay and Sue Reynolds. The next morning saw me head several hundred miles away to another fire.

My first day on that fire, an engine captain recognized me and came over. "I still have the Bible you gave me a couple years ago on a fire," he said. Then he shared how his wife had left him and their two children while he was away on fires. A few days later I heard that a co-worker was struggling in his marriage. I approached him and asked if I could be of any help. He shared that he wasn't sure that his wife would be there when he returned. "I guess I'm here to get away." We talked and I was able to pray with him and give him a New Testament. In all, I shared with four men whose marriages were struggling.

Firefighters, as well as all first responders, have a tragic rate of failed marriages. Often, we try to use our work as an escape from the struggles at home. But, sadly, the time away from home is one of the causes for our struggles in the first place. We love our spouses and children, but at times it seems we love our vocation even more.

†

CHAPTER FIVE

Temptation

Turning Our Back on Ungodly Choices

"'And lead us not into temptation, but deliver us from the evil one.'"

Matthew 6:13

Alligators Come In All Shapes and Sizes

"What's that behind us?" my coworker asked. We were in Mississippi cleaning up after hurricane Katrina. One of our team had discovered an alligator farm and we were looking over 300 of the toothy carnivores from behind a fence.

As we turned to go we spotted a pair of eyes and a snout poking out of the murky waters of an unfenced pond behind us. We had been so busy watching the known danger that we had missed the one that was actually closer to us. As we beat an exit to our vehicle my partner remarked, "There are alligators all around us and they come in all shapes and sizes." That made me think. On the Missionary Ridge Fire in Colorado we lost a firefighter to a falling tree. He was so busy cutting a burning snag that he missed one behind him. Or the firefighters we lost because they were busy watching the fire and drove off an embankment.

Then I thought, "What about my spiritual life?" I'm pretty good about watching out for the big danger areas I face, such as alcohol abuse, illegal drugs, and adultery. But what about the other 'alligators' around me? Am I guarding my eyes from pornography, my heart from bitterness or anger, my spirit from pride? The Bible warns us to, "Be alert and of sober mind. Your enemy the devil prowls around like a roaring lion (alligator?) looking for someone to devour. Resist him, standing firm in the faith," (1 Peter 5: 8-9a).

†

Where's the FOB? Fatality in Texas...?

The fire had taken off quickly — one of hundreds igniting almost simultaneously throughout Texas. Beleaguered crews responded, a line was hurriedly scratched around the flanks as the sun set.

The decision was made to take a bulldozer and strengthen the line before the winds returned in the morning. A Field Observer (FOB), who had walked around the fire, volunteered to lead the dozer. Communication between the FOB and dozer operator was limited. In essence, the operator would watch for the observer's headlamp and follow his lead.

Part way around the fire the duo encountered heavy brush. Periodically, the operator lost sight of his guide only to see the light soon afterward. One time, however, the headlamp didn't reappear. After a few moments, the operator stopped his machine to look around. A light behind him led to a grim discovery — the field observer apparently fell in the thick understory and the dozer went over him. Miraculously, the blade was partially raised and the body passed between the tracks. Still, the observer hovered near death for several weeks in a hospital.

As Christians we are the "light of the world." We're supposed to let our lights shine brightly before men so that they can see Jesus through our actions and glorify God (Matthew 5:14-15). In order to do so we must be very careful how we walk through the "heavy brush" of this world. We can't afford to let any temptation entangle us and cause us to stumble (Hebrews 12: 1-2).

Others are watching us and following our lead. Let's prayerfully let Jesus shine through us and guide others into His wonderful, eternal life!

†

Bitter or Better

"Flight 686 has been delayed another three hours..." Ugh! "I told them it would be quicker if I just drove to the fire!" There are blessings and banes to being a "national resource." I get to go to incidents all over the country, see awesome sights, and meet great people. I also get to sit in airports ad nauseum, miss connecting flights, and eat lots of peanuts and pretzels.

Most of us prefer to drive to the fire, hurricane or other incident rather than fly. You can carry all your gear, have a vehicle when you arrive, and usually get there sooner than if you flew. But on this occasion, I had to fly. The fire wanted me "yesterday." Of course, the delay in Denver made me miss the flight out of San Francisco, which meant I arrived in Arcata at midnight with no transportation to a motel five miles away.

Choices Time:

Choice #1

Do I take 1 Thessalonians 5:18 (NASB) seriously, "In everything give thanks," or grumble at my disappointments? Do I get "bitter" or "better"? Even though the rental cars were all gone and the taxi another thirty minutes away, the Lord graciously had someone share their ride with me and the motel saved the last room. The next morning the fire sent a driver to pick me up.

Choice #2

I can spend the hour ride stewing over my delays or share the love of Jesus with the driver. It turns out the driver was a backslidden brother who was open to coming back to Jesus. For two hours, (yes, when we reached fire camp there weren't any vehicles left and we had to go back to town and rent one), we were able to share together about Peter in the Bible and others of us who had fallen away only to come back even stronger.

The flight home after the fire? More delays, missed flights and airport meals. But if I'd driven, I would never have met that neat pastor in the airport who lost both hands serving Jesus ... Write out the word, "disappointment." Now, change the "d" into an "H." A sure formula for turning bitter to better.

†

Three Strikes and You're ...

All wildland firefighters know that we have some very important things we classify in threes. For example how Fuel-Wind-Topography affect fire behavior or the fire triangle of Heat-Fuel-Oxygen.

As I was reading my Bible this morning, something jumped out at me. Did you know that there is a pattern of threes in the temptations we face? And, that by understanding this pattern we can overcome the temptation? Really, take a look!

When Jesus was tempted in the wilderness (Matthew 4), how many temptations did He face?

- First, the devil tempts Jesus to give in to His hunger pains and show off with a self-serving miracle.
- Second, the devil appeals to Jesus' ego. He urges Jesus to jump off the temple and let everyone see how the Father miraculously saves Him.

- And third, the devil tempts Jesus to settle for immediate gratification by compromising worship of the Father and obedience to the Father's plan in order to get instant kingship of the earth.

Three temptations in three areas of our flesh.

- First, putting God's will second to feeding our "felt needs."
- Second, stoking our egos.
- And third, trying to short cut the path to God's blessings by compromising our worship and obedience of God.

How about Jesus when He was tempted in the Garden of Gethsemane (Matthew 26:39-44)? Three times He was tempted to call off the ridicule, pain and death of the cross. Yet, three times He placed the will of the Father over His own "felt needs," ego, and compromise of the Father's plan and purpose.

When Peter was waiting outside for Jesus' trial after Judas' betrayal, how many times did he give into the temptation to deny Jesus (Matthew 27:69-75)? You're right, three times. How many times did Jesus later ask Peter if he really loved Him (John 21:15-17)? Yup.

When Paul was given a painful "thorn in the flesh" (2 Corinthians 12:7-10 NASB), how many times did He ask God to remove it? Three times. When God said, "No," what temptations did Paul face? To become bitter at God? To give up his faith and obedience to Christ? After all, Paul was a faithful servant of Jesus who "deserved" to be delivered of this affliction. Yet, how did Paul respond to God's negative answer? The Bible says he gave God the glory since God's strength would be even more obvious through his weakness. Paul chose God's will, purpose and glory over his own felt-needs, ego, and instant gratification.

So, what's the point? If these great men of God and even Jesus Himself faced temptations in these areas, won't we? Are you tempted to walk out on your spouse because they're not meeting your "felt-needs"? Does your ego cause you to get bitter because someone else got promoted instead of you? Are you tempted to compromise your worship and witness because you think you can achieve your goals by "short cuts"?

Jesus endured the cross because He knew the Father's plan was the only right one, regardless of the personal cost (Hebrews 12:1-2). Peter realized he had blown it, humbled himself, returned to Jesus and went on to become a great and fruitful servant of God. Paul, as soon as he heard God's, "No," submitted himself to personal trial and humiliation and was used of God then and his words even today as an instrument of God's love and grace.

†

You're the Man!

The man was a legend in the fire business. His expertise was respected far and wide. Only one thing was wrong, he was treading dangerously close to losing his marriage, family and integrity through an inappropriate relationship. Sound familiar? You are his friend, not a close friend, but someone he may listen to. What should you do?

In the Bible a prophet named Nathan faced that dilemma (2 Samuel 12). Except if his friend, the king, didn't like to have his sin pointed out, then Nathan would die. Still, Nathan realized that he had a duty, both to his friend, and more importantly to God. So, he went. After telling King David of a man who had betrayed his neighbor, David replied that the man was guilty and deserved to be put to death. Nathan then looked David in the eye and said, "You're the man."

David had a choice, humble himself, repent, ask forgiveness from God and man, or kill Nathan. Of course, if he killed Nathan he still had God to worry about. David made the right choice. He repented. His testimony is in Psalm 51 and 32:1-7.

All of us are in that picture, one way or another. We're either the man who's on the edge of sin or the friend who needs to talk to him. God loves us and doesn't want us going down a road that will destroy us. So, He sends us a message. Usually it's through another person, although it might be through a traffic stop, radio program, or other means. The point is will we listen, turn from sin and return to God?

✝

Red Flag Warning!

"Red Flag Warning!" These are three words every wildland firefighter understands and is immediately attentive to. Radios all along firelines are turned up to hear the message. "A Red Flag warning has been issued for all of central Interior Alaska for high winds out of the northeast." High winds combined with drought conditions, low humidity and rising temperatures practically shout out to every firefighter, "BEWARE!"

During the 2004 Alaska fire season extreme fire conditions have been the norm not the exception. As the warning goes out, fire managers make sure that each crew receives the update. Every experienced firefighter checks and rechecks his Lookouts, Communications, Escape Routes and Safety Zones. And sure enough, the winds hit and the fires rage. Mile after mile they burn, all over this huge state fires spring to life. Evacuations are called north of Fairbanks; resources are called from the "lower 48" to assist. But thankfully, because of the early warnings and the diligence of each firefighter, no one is trapped or killed.

Our Lord Jesus also issues "Red Flag Warnings" to His workers. BEWARE of becoming those who only do good deeds to be seen by others and not out of love for Christ. BEWARE of immorality and sexual sin of any kind. BEWARE of bitterness springing up in our lives.

Am I as careful to heed these warnings from my Savior as I am warnings on the fireline? Do I turn to God in prayer and ask the Holy Spirit to help me examine my motives? And then do I take time to pause and listen for God's answer? Do I avoid situations that place me in spiritual danger? Do I use the "escape route" from temptation that God promises to provide me in 1 Corinthians 10:13?

As a firefighter I know that ignoring a "Red Flag Warning" can cost me my life. As a Christian can I be any less diligent?

†

Mass Murder

I just received the message. A young man I know has killed and injured a large number of people! With one violent act he destroyed his family, his closest friends, and himself. And, his example will cause others to do the same thing.

Was he a terrorist? A homicidal maniac? A drug crazed gunman? No, he was simply a distraught husband going through a tough time in his life and decided to commit suicide. Wait a minute you say, he only killed himself. Wrong! If you've ever been around such a tragedy you quickly see that many others are killed through this ultimately *selfish* act. His wife, his children, parents, best friends and a host of others die as well. Each one being eaten away by guilt and anguish when one they love rejects them and chooses instead to "bail out" of life. And, adding to the tragedy, he set others up to follow his self-destructive path when they encounter tough times.

Whoa, you say. Isn't that too harsh? Surely the young man didn't mean to act selfishly, to kill and injure so many of his loved ones. No, you're probably right, but that's what he ultimately did, isn't it? Instead of humbly asking for help, he chose to listen to the lies of Satan. The devil told him there was no way out, that this was "best for everyone." But the young man had forgotten that the devil's primary purpose is to "steal and kill and destroy" (John 10:10). He laid aside Jesus' promise that all who are weary and burdened could come to Him and find rest (Matthew 11:28). As each of us knows, even the toughest, darkest hours eventually pass. With God's help we can go through the deep water and come out the other side into the sunshine. The answer is not to try for the coward's way out, the "quick fix," but to ask God and those around us for help. He will stand with us; we can come out of the "valley of the shadow of death" because He will walk through it with us.

What's the bottom line? There's an epidemic of suicide among us today. And it's based on a series of lies. The lie that this trial is too big, that no one understands or cares, that somehow suicide will be better for everyone, that God doesn't care if we murder ourselves, that it's ok to set such a horrible example for others, especially children, around us. These lies come straight from the pits of hell. Satan knows he can't hurt God, so he tries to destroy those God loves, those He gave His life for. Us!

We're all tempted at times, to give up. We all face discouragement and even depression, but remember God's promise in 1 Corinthians 10:13, He will not allow you to be tempted beyond your ability to resist, He will provide a way of escape. When you're struggling, call a pastor, Christian friend, and most of all Jesus. God still has awesome plans for you! With His help you will come through! Are you going to let the devil make a mass murderer out of you? I didn't think so!

†

Dead on the Mountain

I'll never forget when I heard the news. I was driving through Tennessee when the radio announcer broke in with the news. Fourteen firefighters had died on a mountainside in my home state of Colorado. And not just any firefighters, these were Hotshots, Smokejumpers and Helitack. Fourteen of our strongest, most highly trained men and women had perished just hours from my home.

It was July 6, 1994. We didn't have a cell phone in those days, so I searched for the nearest pay phone and called the Forest Service. Yes, I knew Rich, one of the helitack folks, but even those I didn't know personally were part of our fire "family." What had gone wrong? How could this happen?

In a somber mood, I drove on to the church I was to speak in. All kinds of thoughts filled my mind. I could have been on that fire, but the Lord had redirected my steps that summer. What unexpected event had occurred? How were they caught off guard? And most of all, why didn't they go into a safety zone?

Every spring, wildland firefighters are required to attend a Fire Safety Refresher. We review the basic rules of engagement and especially the importance of establishing Lookouts, Communications, Escape Routes, and Safety Zones, (LCES).

As the details of the South Canyon/Storm King tragedy unfolded over the next few weeks and months, one thing became apparent. Even though these were some of the finest wildland firefighters in the United States, they had laid aside the basics of LCES. There were no lookouts posted. There was a breakdown in communication with the dispatchers concerning the upcoming high winds. Their escape route was up a very steep slope, and no adequate safety zones were identified.

When the fifty mph winds aligned with the steep slopes and narrow canyons, disaster was imminent. Looking over all the reports, my heart cringed as I saw the tragedy unfolding. Over and over again I heard the expression, "We didn't feel right about it, but..."

How many times has the same thing happened to you and me? Do we ever enter into a building or start down a hillside with fire below us, and wonder, "Am I missing something here?" Does that little voice inside of us ever say, "Are you sure about this approach?" As firefighters we know we'd better listen and reevaluate our actions!

How about in other areas of our lives? God's Word, the Bible, tells us that we are to hide His Word in our hearts and that it will help us not get caught in the "blowups" of sin (Ps. 119:11). When we have a regular regimen of reading, meditating on, and memorizing Scripture, we're equipping the voice inside us, the Holy Spirit, to sound an alarm and warn us away from the death sin brings. And, when the alarm goes off, it's essential to heed it and rethink our direction.

None of us want to find ourselves, or our friends, in the long funeral procession carrying fallen servants of Christ, "dead on the mountain."

†

Curiosity Killed ...

As the fierce Santa Anna winds pushed the fire onto the stalled fire engine, the windows exploded filling the cab with flame, heat, and smoke. In a matter of moments, four firefighters and one juvenile civilian were seriously burned. One "hitchhiking" civilian tragically perished.

What were two non-firefighters doing "hitchhiking" on the engine during this conflagration? According to the Cal Fire "Green Sheet," which gives a preliminary summary of the event, the civilians were instructed to evacuate the area but instead followed the fire engine back into the fire on their ATV. When the ATV broke down they had to be picked up by the engine crew. As the engine approached a turn-around they found themselves unable to back up due to another civilian on a tractor. At that point the flame front hit them resulting in the injuries and fatality.

If only the residents had followed the evacuation orders! The insistence of the adult to re-enter the fire zone, and allowing the juvenile to follow, cost him his life and caused the juvenile to be critically burned. In addition, that selfish act of curiosity, in combination with the third civilian blocking the engine's egress, caused four firefighters to be burned and their engine destroyed.

Are we sometimes like those civilians? Do we allow our "curiosity" to lure us back into places of danger? Do we allow our "curiosity" to entice us to places that God's Word has told us to evacuate? Pornography, lust, gambling, holding bitterness, are all areas that the Lord tells us to evacuate. If we don't avoid such areas, if we fail to put on God's armor, then we are placing our families and ourselves in imminent danger. Our sin never affects just us. There are others always watching, and when we ignore God's "evacuation orders," they suffer as well.

What area is your curiosity tempting you in? Is there something in your life that God says "Flee?" (2 Timothy 2:22, 1 Corinthians 6:18). God's Word is very clear on this subject. "Flee the evil desires of youth, and pursue righteousness, faith, love and peace, along with those who call on the Lord out of a pure heart," (2 Timothy 2:22). "Flee from sexual immorality. All other sins a person commits are outside the body, but whoever sins sexually sins against their own body," (1 Corinthians 6:18).

†

Who's In Charge Here?

The fire is blowing and going. Thousands of acres of Montana forest are being devoured daily. Our job is to hold a section of line on the north end. I'm the Strike Team Leader. My Division Superintendent is away at the other end of the division. The fire has just jumped our main control line and is moving toward our contingency line. At the moment, I'm in charge of two twenty-person hand crews, two engines, a skidgen, and a water tender.

I have to make a decision fast. I position the crews in a safety zone and begin a burnout off our contingency line. Just as my burnout starts to get established, the wind shifts throwing a spot across the line. We try to encircle the new ignition but heavy smoke drives us back to the safety zone. There I discover two members of the overhead team have arrived and instead of tying in with me, have tried to start crews back into the choking smoke. I try to reason with them but they are insistent. Finally, I lead them and the skidgen back to the spot-fire. The skidgen operator starts throwing up and within minutes the overhead realizes their mistake and follow me out. Soon, the wind shifts again and clears the smoke. Within an hour the spot is extinguished and the line has held.

Our fire line had held, but I'm fuming. These guys had broken the chain of command. They had tried to place my crews in danger. And I had let them bully me into endangering my skidgen operator.

Chain of command is a very important part of forest fire safety. Knowing whom you are responsible to, and for, is necessary for doing the job safely. If someone circumvents that chain, then uneducated and unsafe decisions are going to be made. People are going to be left out of the loop. Wrong assumptions are going to take place.

It's the same in the home and in the church isn't it? If someone has been assigned to a task, is it right to short-circuit the chain of command and assign someone else to do it? Don't we frustrate and confuse people when we fail to follow the chain of command?

Even though church and home situations seem insignificant in comparison to a life-threatening forest fire, aren't they just as important to those involved? The next time we are tempted to overrule those responsible for a task, shouldn't we stop and work with them? We may not understand the situation as well as they do.

Hopefully, we're learning to show respect to those we follow and those whom we lead.

†

Disappointment or His Appointment?

Every firefighter knows that a key word in our business is "flexibility." On our recent deployment to the Florida hurricanes, hundreds of us ran into another "F" word – "frustration." We had been sent to Atlanta for two days of training before being assigned to a disaster zone. However, as the training was ending, another hurricane reared its ugly head. So, instead of being out helping disaster victims, several thousand of us were stuck in a hotel. The agency in charge was overwhelmed by the number of people it had suddenly acquired. As a result, it was having a difficult time implementing the Incident Command System. Tempers began to grow short as direction changed almost hourly. Soon, many began to leave and return home.

After five days we were loaded onto buses for a six-hour ride to Jacksonville. Hope began to spring up. But again, it was hurry up and wait. Hundreds of us milling around while the hurricane played out its fickle dance. Frustration once again began to surface as day after day was filled with mostly meaningless meetings. Finally, someone spoke out what all of us felt, "We've been here almost two weeks without fulfilling our mission."

Then it hit me, as a disciple of Jesus, my mission is whatever He places in my life each day. As I reflected, I realized that everyday He'd been bringing people to my wife and me for counsel, prayer and encouragement. We weren't missing our mission; it just wasn't the one we'd imagined. As we began to look at what the Lord had been doing in and through us, we recognized that our "disappointment" was actually "His appointment." It's funny how just changing one letter can make such a difference.

His Word tells us that He guides the steps of His righteous followers (Psalm 7:23). And I had almost missed the blessing of this special appointment by being tempted to giving in to grumbling in frustration.

The next time I start to feel disappointment, I pray that I will look for His appointment.

"I'm too anointed to be disappointed, too blessed to be depressed!"

†

CHAPTER SIX

Encouragement

Spending Time in Fellowship

"And let us consider how we may spur one another on to-ward love and good deeds, not giving up meeting together, (fellowship) as some are in the habit of doing, but encourag-ing one another—and all the more as you see the Day ap-proaching."

Hebrews 10: 24-25

Is My Inmate Brother Here?

I stepped out of one of "Bob's Johns" and saw an inmate firefight-er walking back to his crew. "Excuse me," I asked, "do you know Richard S?" He looked at me and said, "Yes, he's my cellmate."

Within a few moments I was greeting a brother I had never met. Richard had been given my name by a prison chaplain and had written me a letter several months before. He was involved in fire suppression and felt a call to ministry. I had written him back but this was my first fire since then with inmate crews assigned.

Even though we had never met, we were brothers. Even though at the end of the fire he would return to a cell and I to my home and family, we were co-laborers for the Master.

After I returned home I received a letter from another inmate. He had heard of a tragedy involving one of our church families, and sent a small check to help out. It hit me again. When Jesus talked of visiting Him in prison, I think he had Richard and others like him in mind.

Now I admit I'm not much of a prison minister. I've gone to visit a few friends but not on a regular basis. But I think I need to pray about going more often. After all Jesus and my brothers are there (Matthew 25:34-46).

†

9-1-1 Is No Longer In Service

On August 29, 2005, the Gulf Coast was hit by a devastating hurricane. Katrina not only destroyed miles of homes and businesses, she also knocked out power and phone service.

As I joined hundreds of wildland firefighters responding to Mississippi for relief work, I discovered another side of the disaster I hadn't considered. Strewn amidst the rubble were fire trucks, ambulances and police cars, destroyed by the thirty-foot flood surge. Even if someone in need could call 9-1-1, who would respond? How could a bunch of homeless, station-less, vehicle-less emergency workers come to their aid?

The answer soon became apparent as I passed convoy after convoy of New York, Virginia, and Alabama Police and Fire Departments. These men and women had responded to their brothers' and sisters' needs, not just by sending money, but also by sending themselves. As a result, 9-1-1 was back in service.

As I continued to look around, I saw another miracle. Hundreds of churches, large and small, were rolling in to help. No matter how hard FEMA and other agencies tried, they could only put a dent in the overwhelming need. But it seemed on every street corner a church group set up. Some with clothing, others with food, and still others were helping residents dig out their homes and belongings. Churches from GA, SC, CO, CA deploying on their great mission. Baptists helping Catholics, Methodist and Mennonite serving together, all for the cause of Christ.

Isn't it amazing what we can do when we set our hearts on following God's direction, to consider the needs of others before our own needs or desires? What will we do when 9-1-1 is in danger of going out of service in the lives of those around us?

†

Lonely In a Crowd

There were wildfires raging all over Northern California. Thousands of us had been dispatched from around the United States, going from one fire to another as the overtaxed dispatch system tried to find order in the midst of chaos.

Kind of accidentally, I had become the crew boss of a twenty-person Forest Service hand crew; and it was turning out to be the toughest assignment any of us had ever experienced. From the Modoc to the Klamath National Forest, day after day we climbed steep hillsides and tried to breathe through choking smoke held in by a strong inversion. After the first few weeks, crew members began to develop breathing problems and had to leave. Our sister crew was having the same issue and eventually we lost so many firefighters we had to combine forces just to keep a full twenty person contingent.

Yet, in the midst of the non-stop work and being literally "joined at the hip" with nineteen other firefighters, I became lonely. Loneliness can be a strange thing, striking anyone at any time, even in a crowd. Was it because I felt over my head in responsibilities? Was it because I was feeling the same sickness the rest of the crew was feeling? Was it because I was away from my wife and children? As I reflected, it was probably all of those to a certain extent; but there was something more. It began to dawn on me that I was lonely for fellowship, for other Christians that I could talk with about the Lord, someone I could pray with.

I had heard all the illustrations about the need for fellowship; "A log burns brightly when with other logs, but goes out by itself," "The hand needs the arm, the arm needs the elbow, the elbow needs the...," yet for the first time it really hit home. I was lonely for brothers in Christ.

None of us are wired by God to be "Lone Ranger" Christians. God's Word tells us that there are four things every believer needs on a regular basis. In Acts 2:42 it says, "They (the early Christians) devoted themselves to the apostle's teaching (Bible study), and to fellowship, the breaking of bread (communion) and prayer." Just like Wildland firefighters have a big four, "Lookouts, Communication, Escape Routes and Safety Zones"; every follower of Jesus needs these four essentials. In fact, the primary reason the Fellowship of Christian Firefighters was formed was to meet the need for fellowship every one of us has. Interestingly, the Bible says, "They devoted themselves..." to these essentials. No one had to beg them, nag them, or bribe them with a pot luck dinner. The believers made the effort themselves! God goes on to say, "not giving up meeting together, as some are in the habit of doing, but encouraging one another" (Hebrews 10:25a).

So, what happened on that California hillside? As I realized my need for spiritual fellowship I began to pray, asking God to lead me to other believers. On our mandatory day off I looked up a church in the phone book and talked with the pastor. A few days later I met a helicopter manager who was a believer. And, shortly after that I was able to lead one of my co-workers to Jesus! As I devoted myself to seeking fellowship, the Lord gave it to me! I guess that guy who talked about the logs was right.

†

Where's the Chief?

The modular home was fully involved. Local fire resources were responding and soon the chief was ready to enter the structure and get at the source of the fire. Moments later the call was heard over the radio, "Where's the chief?"

After several minutes of frantic searching, the chief was located, trapped under part of a collapsed floor in the basement. By the time the others were able to safely enter and retrieve him, the chief had perished.

The investigation revealed that the chief had been working in tandem with another firefighter. At one point the other individual had left to check another door. The chief decided not to wait for his return but to enter on his own. As he stepped inside, the floor collapsed and he was trapped.

Is there a lesson here to be learned? Is it smart to enter into dangerous situations on our own? Can I do without back-up?

On a fire or in our private lives it seems wise to "buddy up" with others who will "watch our back" as well as hold us accountable.

In the Bible Jesus sent His disciples out two by two (Luke 9:1-2, 10:1-2). Who are you walking with? Who's got your back? Who is your accountability buddy?

†

Who's Your Lookout?

It was a hot summer's day on a hillside covered with thick brush. Visibility was limited, especially as the crews worked deeper into the drainage. The fire had seemed a nuisance, only one of many burning that July 6th across western Colorado. No one had really thought about posting a lookout; after all, the fire was small and they were all experienced firefighters. Just a few more hours and they could "put a fork in it and call it done."

Unknown to the crews, the fire had crept under the brush below them and was becoming established at the base of the drainage. The fire, wind and topography were all coming into alignment. A disaster was about to unfold.

All wildland firefighters are required to undergo an annual safety refresher. One of the keystones of that refresher is referred to as LCES, meaning Lookouts, Communication, Escape Routes and Safety Zones. Yet, every year fatalities occur because of our neglecting one or more of these "big four."

The Bible tells us to be lookouts for each other; "...remember this: Whoever turns a sinner from the error of their way will save them from death and cover over a multitude of sins" (James 5:20). We must keep a lookout for things that will harm us; and those around us. If we don't, we will miss the smoldering sin which will crawl around in the underbrush of our life until it aligns itself and explodes.

That day on Storm King Mountain someone finally did notice. Not a lookout, for there was none posted, but someone carrying water to the crew. His shout of warning saved many, but it was too late for fourteen men and women who perished.

Who's your lookout? Who have you given permission, "appointed" to shout out a warning when things in your life are "coming into alignment" for disaster?

†

I Hated You!

It was almost embarrassing. I had just arrived on the Angora fire at South Lake Tahoe when a firefighter came running up to me and gave me a big hug. "Rick," he said, "I'm so glad to see you!"

As we began to talk, he explained how he had "hated" me when we had worked on a fire a couple of years before. "I tried to avoid you because your presence was a constant reminder of how I needed to come to Jesus," he said. "But finally, I gave my life to the Lord!" He proceeded to keep encouraging me, asking me to forgive him for his previous attitude. Which, of course I did.

The interesting thing was that I was only on the Angora Fire for one day. The winds had died and so had the fire. They were already releasing resources when I arrived. Yet, while I was there I had the opportunity to give away several *Answering the Call* New Testaments as well as pray with two of the Teen Challenge camp helpers.

Do you ever wonder if God is using you? Do you ever feel that people "hate" you without cause? The Bible tells us that the Holy Spirit living in us is the "aroma of Christ." To those who are resisting God, we are the smell of death. To those who yield to His love and respond to His call, we are the "fragrance of life" (2 Corinthians 2:14-16).

Sometimes folks don't like me because I've got a bad attitude or have acted like a jerk. But other times I have to realize that it's not me they "hate," it's the Spirit of God living in me. My job is to keep loving them, praying for them and living a life that will attract them to Jesus.

As I left my new brother, I was truly encouraged by our time of fellowship. And, I was reminded not to be discouraged when someone's first reaction to me and my faith is negative. God isn't finished with me, or them, yet.

†

Where's Your Safety Zone?

In the summer of 2003, two young wildland firefighters tragically perished, only three minutes from their Safety Zone. And, even worse, they were headed away from it when they were overrun by the fire!

As they were dropped onto the fire, a safety zone was pointed out from the air. Apparently, they never walked to it or flagged a route that they could follow if the fire blew up. They knew that the "18 Situations That Shout Watch-Out" and "Standard Fire Orders" were very clear about identifying, walking, and flagging an adequate Escape Route and Safety Zone. "But this is only a short-term assignment, one that will take an hour or less," I'm sure they thought. Then, seven hours later, when the fire raced up the adjoining draw, they frantically searched in vain for the Safety Zone.

Where is your Safety Zone? Most of us as fire/EMS personnel are well-trained and confident. We know that cutting corners on safety will ultimately come back to bite us. And yet, sometimes we take chances with our eternal life that we'd never risk on a fire assignment. For instance, have each of us personally asked Jesus Christ to forgive our sins and trusted Him to do it? Have we committed ourselves to obey Him each day and asked Him to fill us continually with His Holy Spirit? Or, are we counting on doing that later, if things get tough? Some firefighters see the fire racing up the hillside and have time to look for a Safety Zone. But many others can't see the fire until it's too late. Then, because they didn't establish their Safety Zone ahead of time, they run aimlessly into flames of certain death. Some people have a last second chance to receive Christ, but most find death comes unexpectedly.

During a typical wildland fire assignment, a radio call goes out inquiring if LCES (Lookouts, Communication, Escape Routes, Safety Zones) are in place. On a structure fire it might be a call for PAR (accounting for all your personnel). That's not a bad idea for our daily lives as well. Are we reading our Bibles each morning, talking to God throughout the day and seeking the Holy Spirit to fill and lead us? Are we staying involved in fellowship? Why wait until life blows-up and makes a run to destroy us?

✝

Tragedy in a Meadow

It was a crazy fire season in Texas. Multiple grass fires day after day, week after week. On this incident there was a combination of agencies and apparatus. They had entered a gated pasture and begun suppression when a wind event threw everything into chaos. Trucks were stuck in ditches, others tried to back out only to collide with each other. Some firefighters abandoned their rigs and sought shelter in other vehicles. Only one truck seemed to maintain a form of situational awareness. Its crew laid out a hose to protect the engine and burned out around it.

In a few minutes the winds died and the crews began to assess what had happened. Damaged and disabled engines seemed to be everywhere. Then they made a tragic discovery; one of their crew members lay dead in a ditch. He had apparently been run over by a retreating vehicle who didn't even know they had hit him. A sense of horror and grief overcame the crews.

In the days that followed, many questions were asked and re-asked. Who was in charge of the strike team? Where was the escape route? Why did the communication between the engines fail? Why was the deceased out of his engine on foot?

As we reviewed this terrible tragedy, the similarities with life became apparent. Who is in charge of our life? If each of us thinks we're our own "captain," then we begin the chain of events which lead to disaster. Where is our "escape route?" If we are counting on coming up with a plan for eternal life "on the fly," then how reliable will that be on the final day? If we aren't in communication with the One who knows all, and with our fellow crew members while on this journey of life with its perils, what prevents us from disaster as the world around us disintegrates into chaos? And if we try to get out of the truck and go on our own way, what is there to protect us?

God's Word, the Bible, gives us an "Incident Action Plan" that won't let us down. First, we need someone who can direct our lives through the "valley of the shadow of death" and bring us out safely. That person is Jesus! He wants to lead us by His Holy Spirit and His Word in the good times and the bad (John 14:26, John 16:13). Second, our "Escape Route" and "Safety Zone" is no less than our faith and trust in Him. If we have predetermined that we will follow Him as our Lord, He will not only guide us, He will protect us and lead us into eternal life (Psalm 23:4-6)! His communication channel with us is simply prayer; both talking to and listening to Him moment by moment. Be careful not only to have your "radio" programmed to transmit; be sure it also is set to receive and obey (Philippians 4:6-8). Checking in frequently with our fellow crew members is essential as well. Church and Bible studies, at work and at home help keep us on track (Acts 2:42). And of course, setting out on our own and leaving our crew is never wise. God instructs us to not to give up meeting together with other believers who can encourage us and help us find our bearing when we lose our way (Hebrews 10:25).

†

That Guy, Lord?

"That guy, Lord; you want me to be friends with that guy?" It was the beginning of fire season. I was in the Forest Service office doing early season paperwork, hoping to get out in the field as soon as possible. Then I saw "Joe," trying to fill in paperwork. He was awkward, shy and looked totally out of place. He was dressed wrong, his skin was discolored from some type of birth mark, and he just didn't fit in. And yet, I had an immediate nudge from the Holy Spirit to be his friend. Have you ever felt the Lord leading you to someone you didn't want to meet?

I think a big part of my hesitancy was my own insecurity. I was trying to "fit in" myself and still had this Junior High mentality that if I hung around "un-cool" people I would be considered "un-cool." I was a pretty new Christian and just beginning to understand that my self-worth and identity comes from Jesus and not from the crowd. Still, I did remember that my Boss, Jesus, chose to hang out with folks that the crowd rejected. (Luke 7:34). So, I went over and introduced myself to Joe. Later that morning I volunteered to help him learn to drive a stick shift pickup truck. (What do they teach guys back in the East☺?)

During the day I found out that Joe was a Christian, my brother in Christ. I invited him to church and discovered that he was also a phenomenal singer. For the rest of the summer we saw each other at least weekly, and soon others found out that despite first impressions, Joe was a good guy and hard worker.

Have you ever felt you were the one others didn't want to meet? It's awkward entering a new environment isn't it? Joining a new crew or being assigned to a new station can be strange at first. Remember, those around you may feel unsure about how to approach you. Be patient and let Jesus shine through you. And, let's help each other not be afraid of being a friend to the "unlovely," or to "tax collectors and sinners"!

†

When a Good Man Dies

In the 1970's a Denver fireman sensed God impressing upon him a special vision. This vision would take years of hard work and personal sacrifice. I'm sure he questioned, "Who am I to do such a thing?" He wasn't a preacher, chaplain or "super saint." In fact, not long ago he had been a drinker and womanizer. Only by the grace of God and some caring friends had he come to know the Savior.

Still the vision persisted. So, even as he moved from Captain to Assistant Chief, he began meeting with other firefighters for fellowship and Bible study. One day, while at a fire conference in Memphis, TN, he met another Christian fireman named Bob. As God would have it, Bob had the same vision, only larger. As they talked and prayed, the vision began to take shape. What would happen if every shift in every fire station offered an opportunity for Bible study and fellowship?

So began the seminal vision for the Fellowship of Christian Firefighters. Duncan Wilkie and Bob Crum realized that God was calling them, not because of their great ability but their availability. Not because of their wisdom, but their humility and willingness to trust and obey Him. God further developed the vision by bringing John Barker alongside to handle the administrative needs. As the vision became known, men and women around the world rose to embrace it. It was truly God's vision!

God has promoted Duncan and Bob to a new assignment; that of an "overhead" position in our Father's house! So what happens when a good man dies? Perhaps we can look at the answer from several angles.

First, some will object to the term "good man." Didn't our Lord make it clear that no one is really "good" except God (Mark 10:18). Of course He did. Still, when we become new persons by receiving Jesus as Savior and Lord, He places His righteousness on us (2 Corinthians 5:21). So, in that sense we might say someone becomes "good" by God's grace.

Second, what happens on earth when a "good" man dies? Sadly, they don't always get recognized. Thousands of godly men and women have passed seemingly unnoticed into heaven. Yet, their heritage remains in the lives of their families, co-workers and those they influenced for Jesus. Sometimes, we're as fortunate as Duncan and Bob; ministries we helped build continue to influence souls for Christ after we're gone.

Third, when a man or woman who's been made "good" by God takes their final breath on this earth, they discover what Jesus meant when He said their reward in heaven is great! Truly, no eye has seen or ear heard or have we even imagined what God has prepared for those who love Him (1 Corinthians 2:9)! The apostle Paul said he looked forward to "depart and be with Christ, for that is very much better" (Philippians 1:23b NASB). He enters into an eternity of joy, peace and face to face fellowship with Jesus!

So, what happens when a good man dies? He leaves behind a legacy in the lives around Him and enters into the very presence of God, his Savior!

The ultimate question then is this. What about those of us who haven't answered that last tone out yet? Isn't it obvious that the Captain of our Souls still has work for us to do? To continue to build on the vision that He has given us, until He calls us home!

†

A Winning Team (That Almost Lost)

The call came only minutes after I went available for dispatch. I was heading to Washington State as a Strike Team Leader for Engines (STEN). Now a STEN is usually responsible for five to seven engines, often less. However, during this assignment I was ultimately given responsibility for a myriad of engines, a dozer, a 20-person hand crew, and even a masticator. I've told the story in a previous issue of how the Lord used that experience to humble and "re-align" my priorities.

But the "rest of the story" is as follows. I was immediately assigned to cover an assortment of isolated structures surrounded by thick timber. The fire was steadily moving toward the cabins. I felt bewildered, where should I start? In my indecisive mood, those I was leading felt frustrated as well. We were on the verge of being a "losing team."

Finally, after prayer and more than a few anxious moments, I began to assess the strengths and weaknesses of my assigned resources. As I leaned on their expertise, and assigned them accordingly, we began to jell as a team. I started making decisions based on their input along with my experience and training. Then, as things slowed a bit I went deeper in my conversations with each crew. What did they hope to accomplish on this assignment? Did they have certain blanks in their "task books" (a log of specific experience requirements they must fulfill to reach the next level) that I could help them with? For one it was the experience of calling in helicopter water drops, for another it was to be my trainee as a STEN. Some of the engines were from another part of the country and this might be their only opportunity to be "signed off" on certain tasks. They had been waiting years for a "western fire" assignment. What could I do to help them achieve their goals?

Over the next two weeks, my "losing" team became a "winning" one. Overhead began stopping by to tell me what a cohesive group we had. We hated to leave each other when we "timed out."

What caused things to change? Of course, it started with fervent prayer. I'm not ashamed to say I shot up many petitions to the Lord, including "HELP." But, after that, I believe it grew out of a willingness to listen to my resources, assess and utilize their strengths, and help them achieve their personal goals even as we achieved those of the Incident Commander.

In some ways, I guess I became a "servant-leader." Isn't this at least part of what Jesus was talking about when He told the disciples that to be a leader, you have to serve those you lead? (Matthew 20: 20-28).

When God's word tells us to honor the individual gifts of other believers around us (1 Corinthians 12), doesn't that involve taking the time to identify those gifts, value them and utilize them?

"Lord, please help me learn to be a servant leader like you; at work and in your church. I don't have all the answers. I need my brothers and sisters to help me make wise decisions so that we can be a 'winning team'."

†

I Love This Job!

"Why do you guys like to fight fire so much?" my Forest Service co-worker asked. "Why do you jump at the chance to work sixteen-hour days, breathe tons of smoke, sleep on the ground and eat out of a box for two or three weeks?" Good question. Why do first responders run toward what everyone else is running away from?

I started mumbling something about the "H's and O's" (hazard pay and overtime), but my supervisor corrected me in mid-sentence. "It's not about the money," he said, "It's more than that. You become part of a very special family. Every fire assignment is like a family reunion."

He was right. After you've gone on a few wildland fires you begin to see the same faces showing up. You recognize the division supervisor or line medic. You even look for specific food catering units. (These days we only eat out of a box for a few shifts; then we get a "hot can" or even semi-trucks which turn into kitchens ... truly a life of luxury!) The early mornings around the ten-gallon coffee urn or warming heater become times of renewing friendships and trading stories of the last big incident. "Do you remember when ...?"

On an incident we lay aside differences of race, agency or background and join together as a team to accomplish the task we were called for. We have each other's back. We have one task; to do our job the best we can and bring everyone home safe! As a result of being united in one purpose and sharing the same hardships, we become family. When one suffers, we all do. When one succeeds, we all rejoice!

I love my job!

What if our "Christ Incident" becomes the same type of assignment? What if when we come together we see each other as family? As co-workers reaching out to a lost world with the good news of Jesus? What if we lay aside race, denomination or background and work together to fulfill our task of extinguishing the fires of hell that are destroying souls around us? Wouldn't we become a "family" that loves to come together? The Bible says that without a common vision or mission, people waste their efforts. (Proverbs 29:18) But a team of committed workers can destroy Satan's strongholds! (Matthew 16:18, 1 John 4:4). As I assume my role as a follower of Jesus, working with my "family" to accomplish God's will, I'm willing to share hardships until we meet our Lord's objectives. I truly love this job!

What about the co-worker who asked the question about why we loved fighting fire? She decided to sign up for the next fire dispatch. Unfortunately, it was twenty-eight days in the most difficult terrain and smokiest conditions our crew had ever experienced. Half way through the assignment she told me that when she got home she was getting married, having babies and raising a family. And she did! That sounds a lot harder to me.

†

Heroes of the Faith
Retirement, What Retirement?

Bill and Ann Babb

I was drinking my coffee and reading the Bible in my "downtown office" (McDonalds) when they came in. The first thing I noticed was the "Dallas Fire Department-Retired Chief" hat he was wearing. Taking an *Answering the Call* (ATC) New Testament from my pack, I went over and introduced myself. Within a few moments I realized that Bill and Ann Babb were both followers of Jesus. That began a several-year friendship.

Not long after our first meeting, Bill asked for a case of 50 ATCs to distribute at a fire conference in Texas. We gladly loaded them in his vehicle and prayed that God would use each copy to draw firefighters to Jesus. After the positive response he received, Bill began to ask for more cases. It seemed he would stop at each fire station he passed and take a copy to the chief, offering more copies if they desired. The last time Bill was able to come our way he and Ann had just reached 90 years of age. "Rick," he said, "we go up to the station using our walkers and wearing my hat. Not one station has refused the Bibles"! Bill and Ann Babb, "heroes of the faith."

*Just over a year ago, Bill answered his final call. This year two friends of the Babbs showed up at my "office." They asked for a case of ATCs so they could carry on the ministry!

Don and Josie Biggs

"Rick, I need more ATCs and *Peacemaker* New Testaments!" Don and Josie Biggs were on the road again. Don is a retired fireman from the Washington DC Fire Department. As he and Josie travel through the southeastern United States to visit friends and family they stop at each station they pass. Like the Babbs, they go in and offer copies of ATCs and Encouragers to those on duty. In addition, they interact with law enforcement officers they come in

contact with, offering them copies of the police version of the New Testament, the "Peacemaker."

What do the Babbs and Biggs have in common? They've never met, never gone to seminary, and aren't professional chaplains. They're Christians who realize that the Great Commission (Matthew 28:18-20) of Jesus applies to all of us. They realize that retirement from the fire service does not mean retirement from our Lord's service. They understand that whether we're 90 or 19, we have the privilege and responsibility to carry the good news of salvation through Jesus Christ to "all." They are true "Heroes of the Faith"!

By the way, copies of the *Answering the Call* and *Peacemaker* New Testaments are available at no cost from Rick Barton Ministries, P.O. Box 1155, Gunnison, CO 81230. The *Peacemaker* is still in print and Harper Collins plans to re-release the ATC in December of 2017!

†

CHAPTER SEVEN

A Time of Laughter

Finding Joy

"There is a time for everything, and a season for every activity under the heavens ... and a time to laugh ..."

Ecclesiastes 3: 3, 4

OOPS!

My shift was over and I had drained and parked the engine. Just as I was enjoying a good home-cooked meal the phone rang. "Barton, go to the garage and get your engine, then head up toward Lake City. Someone turned in a smoke report and we want to hit it tonight while it's still small."

Oh well, it was the middle of fire season, and the H's and O's

(hazard pay and overtime) would be a blessing. So, I threw on my Nomex clothes and headed back to the Forest Service garage. Loading my gear on the engine, I picked up my co-worker and off we went. Adrenaline kicking in we began to plan our strategy and even how we might spend this paycheck; a canoe, a new fishing rod, etc.

Before long, the boss called on the radio telling us where to leave the pavement. As we jostled up a pretty rugged four-wheel drive road, I was impressed how well the engine was doing. It was almost as if it wasn't loaded with 250 gallons of waaaa...! Did I mention we drained the tank?

Oops! Ever feel like a real, Class A dummy? Here I am re-sponding to a wildfire with a type 6 brush engine and suddenly realizing I had forgotten to refill the water tank. Being young, dumb and scared to death of my FMO, I didn't say anything and started looking like mad for a stream to draft from. Nothing.

It seemed forever before we arrived on scene. The boss ap-proached the truck. "Can't do it" he said. "It's up a pretty nasty hillside and we can't safely get to it tonight. Besides, it's in the rocks and not going anywhere. You guys head back to town."

Not only has Jesus told us "Be dressed in readiness, and *keep* your lamps lit" (Luke 12:35 NASB). But the Apostle Paul also admonishes us to "be prepared in season and out of season" to share the truth of Jesus and His salvation (2 Timothy 4:1-2). I don't know about you, but I don't want to let my Savior down by showing up with an "empty tank" and not being ready to serve and share the Gospel. I want to refill daily by reading His Word, being in prayer, and yielding to the Holy Spirit's control.

What's that you ask, did I ever tell my FMO about the empty tank? I can't exactly remember. It's been thirty years or so, and maybe he's reading this article...

†

Certificate for Whining

It was the call most of us in the "Lower 48" long for! "Can you go to Alaska for an assignment?" The next night when I arrived in Fairbanks; it was midnight and the sky was still light. Smoke was everywhere. The Black Spruce prevalent in Alaska had truly proven to be "gas on a stick." Some fires had already burned over one million acres.

I was assigned to work in the joint information center of the Alaska Fire Service. Our job was to coordinate media, concerned public, and government entities requests for information about the fires. We had queries from all over the world and visits from the Governor and a United States Senator.

As my month-long assignment wound down we began to prepare *Certificates of Appreciation* for the many folks who had assisted the fire operation. One of our trainee information officers developed a striking certificate with a picture of the fires encompassing the text. I *subtly* hinted that I would certainly appreciate one myself.

As the day of my departure approached, the certificate was presented to me! It was signed by the Alaska Interagency Coordination Center Manager and definitely suitable for framing. Imagine my dismay when I read the inscription,

"Presented to Rick Barton for Complaining Incessantly About Not Having a Certificate of Appreciation, Happy Now?"

I'm pretty sure they were kidding?

Well, it does hang on my wall, as a reminder that our whining and badgering may eventually bring us awards, but are they really the ones we want?

"...give thanks in all circumstances; for this is God's will for you in Christ Jesus" (1 Thessalonians 5:18).

†

Saved By the Leaf Blowers!?

It was the end of October; the 2000 forest fire season had finally come to an end. After dispatches from Texas to Montana, I had stored the red bag for the winter. Then the phone rang once again. This time the fires were in North Carolina and Tennessee.

On the way out the door, my fire management officer yelled, "Don't forget, Barton, that stuff burns in the rain." Surely not, I thought.

A day later I arrived in Asheville, picked up an Alaska smoke-jumper as a trainee and drove to the fire. Before long we heard a strange sound coming toward us through the hardwoods. The Mescalero Hotshots burst into view with leaf blowers and swatters! Our jaws hit the ground. What kind of fireline was this?

But it worked. The fire was being carried by leaf litter, and the blowers cut a swath quickly and effectively with minimal resource damage.

I guess we learned a lesson that day. Different conditions call for different methods. Whether we're starting a conversation with an unbeliever, choosing a style of music to reach our audience, or picking a spot to hold a Bible study, we need to be prayerful and flexible in our approach. As someone once told me, "God's principles and truths never change, His methods always do!"

The hotshots were stopping the fire, more quickly and efficiently with leaf blowers than Pulaski's and combi-tools ever could. Maybe meeting in a coffee shop might be more effective in reaching our unsaved and unchurched friends than using the church's facilities, who knows? ... **Oh yeah,** that stuff really does burn in the rain!

†

A Merry Heart Is Good Medicine

Have you ever tried really hard to be serious and failed miserably?

I was the crew boss in charge of mopping up a one hundred-acre forest fire. My position was above the crew on the adjoining hillside where I could direct them to spot fires. At the end of shift I began heading cross-country to the main trail back to the vehicles. Instead of following the flagging I took a "short cut." I soon reached the main trail and started hiking out.

The problem was, I kept coming across fallen trees across the trail. Trees that weren't there that morning. After a half-hour of struggling over the downfall, I pulled out my compass. It too was messed up. It said I was headed away from the vehicles and directly into the wilderness area. Oops!

What about the time we were in the midst of the Colorado Wildfire Academy? The lead Information Officer for our incident management team was teaching a classroom full of budding trainees. Suddenly, one of the students noticed the sign on the door said "Infoamation Officer." The instructor had goofed up the title for her own class.

Or the time on fire patrol when I got turned around in "Lost Canyon" and called in a smoke *north* of town that turned out to be the cement factory *south* of town. A fact I discovered after I had already sent everybody *north* to find the "fire."

What do we do? How should we react in those moments? I think the only thing appropriate is to humble ourselves and laugh! We're human and we goofed. No one was hurt, only our egos. I think the Lord may allow us to "discover" that no matter how much of a legend we are in our own minds, we really are fallible. And realizing our weaknesses is not necessarily a bad thing. It reminds us that we are still learning, and to have grace towards the mistakes of others. Proverbs 17:22 tells us that a merry heart is good medicine. What better way to achieve a merry heart than to laugh at ourselves?

Of course, I confessed my mistakes to my co-workers ... six or seven years later.

Macedonian Christians Spotted In Mississippi!
Count It All Joy

While serving on two hurricane relief details in Mississippi, I ran across a group of "Macedonian" Christians. The interesting thing was that these folks had probably never been in Macedonia. Some had probably never even heard of it. But they were doing exactly what the Macedonians did in 2 Corinthians 8:1-5. The Bible tells us "Out of the most severe trial, their overflowing joy and their extreme poverty welled up in rich generosity."

Apparently, these biblical Macedonian believers were in the midst of really tough times. Yet, when word came that the Jerusalem Christians were suffering hardship, they took up a sacrificial offering and "pleaded" with the apostles for the privilege of helping. In Bay St. Louis, MS, where hurricane Katrina reached landfall, terrible devastation occurred. Block after block, mile after mile stretched forth with only foundations of homes and businesses remaining. Yet, in the midst of all this I came across Lakeshore Baptist Church. All that remained of their sanctuary was the steeple propped up in the parking lot. But, to my amazement, the church members had set up tables and were serving food and clothing to their neighbors. These southern Mississippi residents who lost all their material belongings became honorary "Macedonians." And, when our wildland firefighters were withdrawn after eight weeks, guess who volunteered to man our food, water, and ice distribution station?

During times of stress, people can become "better" or "bitter." These believers chose the "better" path. Through the power of the Holy Spirit they decided to "count it all joy" when the tough times came and became the light of Christ to all around them. When we read stories of great people in the Bible, do you ever wonder if they are "super Christians" or just regular folks like us?

In Bay St. Louis, Waveland, and Pearlington, a bunch of "ordinary" Christians took God at His word and gave beyond their ability for the glory of God. Can we dare do anything less?

The Surprise Birthday

It was the end of a hard week of fighting fire in Northern California. The "Siege of 87" had called hundreds of crews together to attack over a thousand new starts in the northwest. I had just become the crew boss of our Forest Service regulars. Disembarking from our helicopter transport, we were forming our strike team on a ridge top.

"Hey Rick," one of my crew members yelled at me, "Is today your birthday?" "No," I responded, "my birthday was five months ago." "Close enough," she said and began yelling to everyone that it was my birthday. Soon sixty or so tired, dirty smoke chasers were singing *Happy Birthday* at the top of their lungs. I turned beet red in my denials, but it did no good.

Of course, that started it. Every few days and eventually at least once every fire, we chose someone to have a surprise birthday. We would whisper the "big day" to the waitress and join in a rousing chorus when the cake and candle appeared.

Is it "OK" to laugh on a fire crew? Of course! It's a necessary relief valve. How about in our Christian life and service? Isn't it just as important to enjoy our walk with Christ? The Bible says that the "Joy of the Lord is your strength" (Nehemiah 8:10). Of course, joy isn't all laughing and hijinks, but it does certainly include a good hearty bellyacher once in a while.

When's the last time you had a good, godly laugh? When's the last time you put down your "spiritual" look and had some good, clean fun?

✝

The Lynching of the Crew Boss

"Hey crew boss, we've got a problem!" one of my crew shouted from the back of the bus. "Take a look at our time sheets and compare them to the White River Crew!"

I was serving as crew boss on a twenty-person Forest Service fire crew in California when I was almost "lynched." Unknowingly, I had been recording less time each day on the Crew Time Reports (CTR's) than the other crew in our strike team. As a new crew boss, I had been extra careful with the CTR's, rounding the times down rather than up like the other crew. After a couple weeks on the assignment, the difference was growing. Wildland firefighters don't make a great hourly wage and count on overtime to pay the bills at home; and I had just cut into those hours!

Two things can get a crew boss in big trouble on a fire assignment; putting your crew into unnecessary danger and messing up their time. When you mess up on one of those basics, you're in trouble; the crew starts pulling out the rope!

As a Christian I have to be careful about the basics as well. In Acts 2:42 (NASB), we are told the believers, "devoted themselves to the apostles' teaching (Bible study) and to fellowship, to the breaking of bread, and to prayer."

Periodically we need to check our spiritual CTR's and compare them with God's plan and will for our lives. Adhering to these four "basics" will keep ourselves and those who follow us out of danger, and make our "CTR's" balance out!

So, what happened in California? Well, after huddling with the Strike Team Leader, I was able to adjust our schedule for the next week and make up the time. No "neck tie" party that time.

"Lord Jesus, please help me to pay attention to the 'basics' in my life and not cut Your time short!"

✝

CHAPTER EIGHT

God of Grace

Serving a Lord of Grace, Mercy, and Hope

"The Word became flesh and made his dwelling among us. We have seen his glory, the glory of the one and only Son, who came from the Father, full of grace and truth."

John 1:14

May Day! May Day!

"May Day! May Day!" my radio suddenly crackled! The universal call of someone in distress came across the Forest Service frequency loud and clear. The problem was I had no idea who was calling, what their emergency was, or even where they were. Even though the call was being picked up on our frequency, they apparently couldn't hear us responding.

With a prayer for wisdom, I called the police dispatch center and they joined me in trying to locate the party in need. Search and rescue units were assembled, and after discussion, dispatched to a popular hang-gliding area. Before long the injured party was located and aid administered.

I can only imagine the feeling of helplessness the person on the other end of the radio must have felt. Calling out for help and not knowing if anyone could hear them. Was the radio working? Was help on the way?

Sometimes I feel that way. I'm in trouble, I know it, and call out to God for help. Yet, it feels as if there's no answer. Is my "radio" working? Does God hear me? Is help on the way? When I start wondering, I remember Daniel (Daniel 10:12-14). Daniel is assured that God heard his cry and initiated a "search and rescue" operation from the minute his humble prayer was heard. Our God has promised to never leave us or forsake us, (Hebrews 13:5), He promises that nothing can ever separate us from Him (Romans 8:35-39). Wow, what a blessing and assurance!

So, shout out that "May Day" to the Savior, He never tunes us out.

†

To Tell the Truth!

The phone rang; it was my boss. I knew it meant trouble, probably the end of my firefighting career!

I was a seasonal worker for the Forest Service and couldn't get enough of firefighting. In fact, I had started my own twenty-person fire crew, just to get out more. My regular job was running a TSI (timber stand improvement) crew, but I wanted to fight fire.

The problem started when my fire crew was dispatched to Wyoming. Unexpectedly, I was told I couldn't go. I was needed to run my TSI crew. It was hard enough to get twenty people together on short notice and now they were keeping me home. As I scrambled to contact my firefighters, one of the District officers came by my desk. "Barton," he said, "you'd better get a full crew together, and I don't care how you do it."

Rather than prayerfully appeal my case to my bosses, I panicked. I basically went out on the street and recruited untrained men who needed work. This was totally against the rules, but I was desperate. The crew left with its minimum complement, and I sighed with relief as the plane left the ground. Still, worries haunted me. What would happen if my deception was discovered?

"Rick," my boss said over the phone, "someone checked your crew and discovered some men without Red Cards. They're sending the crew back and the Ranger wants to talk to you in the morning." Well, my hopes came crashing down. What should I do? Try to worm out of this or face the music. It was a long night.

The next morning, I met with the Ranger. I had made my decision after much prayer. "I panicked and broke the rules," I confessed. "I'm ready to resign and take my punishment." After more discussion, the Ranger accepted my apology but not my resignation. "You've learned a hard lesson," he said, "and don't expect any more fire calls." I left his office saddened by his last comment but with the confidence I had done the right thing. The Bible tells us to confess our sins (James 5:16, 1 John 1:9) and not to lie (Colossians 3:9).

Unexpectedly, other fire managers came to my aid and a few weeks later my crew and I were dispatched again. In fact, the Maranatha (Come Quickly Lord Jesus) Fire Crew went out several more times around the region. And, thirty years later, I continue to fight fires.

Looking back, I'm grateful for a God who wouldn't let me get away with deception and a Ranger who would forgive.

We serve a God of grace. He is there to forgive, we just need to believe and confess.

†

The "Double-Tithe" Fire

The phone rang, "Rick, we need you as a safety officer in Norwood, now!" Thus, began the saga of what I call "The Double-Tithe Fire." A quick check of my gear, load the Explorer, and off I went.

"Can we afford this?" That morning my wife and I had been relaxing before church and going over a list of needs from students going on mission trips. My fire season hadn't started yet; I'd been busy with ministry and hadn't made myself available. As a result, any giving over our tithe would be a stretch; and the total for all the needs was twice as much. Fortunately, being married to a godly wife insures that we don't just look at our own resources. After prayer we decided to double our giving.

Less than five minutes later the call came. Usually early season fires in Western Colorado are short duration, wind-driven events. I figured I'd be home in a day or two. Well, as the Lord would have it, the fire stretched out for a week and after working seventy-nine hours, the giving was covered and even some left over. God's promises are always certain. His grace and mercy are forever.

"Give, and it will be given to you. They will pour into your lap a good measure—pressed down, shaken together, *and* running over. For by your standard of measure it will be measured to you in return" (Luke 6:38 ... NASB).

†

How Fast Is Your Car?

"I need to pray with you!" the firefighter said, with a real sense of urgency.

I had just finished speaking at a chapel service for the Arizona Wildfire & Incident Management Academy. Fifty or so had shown up and the Lord had done some neat things. Justin Unger and the worship team did a wonderful job. Chaplain Sam, Public Affairs Officer Ken Frederick, and Darrell Willis, the deputy IC had gotten things going strong. When my time came, I shared the Gospel.

After I finished the message and had given those in attendance a chance to respond, the group began to break up. Some left for dinner; others were praying or enjoying fellowship. Suddenly this young man approached me. "I need to pray with you," he said. Then he told me a most remarkable story. The Lord had touched him during the service but he had decided to leave without making a commitment. As he reached his car and turned on the ignition, a song came on the radio. The words went something like, "You can get in your fast car and drive away, or you can come back and change your life forever!" He came back and yielded his life to Jesus. What A God of grace we serve!

Isn't it amazing that God loves us so much that He not only sent His Son to die for us, but that He will do whatever it takes to give us a chance to respond. Out of all the things He could be doing, He decided to play a love song for a child He wanted to come home.

What about you and me? Are we going to drive away or come home?

✝

Wait, Come Back!

Suddenly it hit me; I had missed the most important point of all! Recently, I was assigned to a wildland fire in N. California. Shortly after arriving in camp a man noticed my Fellowship of Christian Firefighter t-shirt and asked what being a Christian Firefighter meant. As I answered, he began sharing that even though he had been raised in a Christian home he now felt that all religions were equal and our job was to simply pick one and we'd be fine, as long as we were sincere, etc.

We talked for quite a while and I shared with him the uniqueness of Jesus, His claims and offer of salvation. I urged Him to realize that Jesus was either a liar, because He said He was God and knew He really wasn't, a lunatic, because He thought He was God but wasn't, or Lord, because He in fact is all He claimed to be. Jesus couldn't be just a good teacher or prophet because of who He said He was, the only son of God and the only way to heaven (paraphrasing former atheist C.S. Lewis).

Our conversation was cordial and ended with no apparent progress being made on my part. The next morning, he was gone and suddenly it hit me. I had missed the most important point. If any religion was sufficient to get us to heaven, if doing our best would suffice, then why did Jesus have to come and die? There were plenty of religions at the time, lots of folks doing their best, but only His death to pay for our sins could restore us to fellowship with God. As Galatians 2:21 says, "I do not set aside the grace of God, for if righteousness could be gained through the law, Christ died for nothing." I wished I could have had another chance.

As I shared my failure with a brother in Christ on the fireline, he reminded me that the Holy Spirit gives us the words to share at the time, and that we can pray and trust that He will bring someone else along to finish what I began. I know he's right, but I pray that next time I won't forget this basic truth: There is no other way to come to God except through the shed blood of His Son, Jesus!

✝

Off the Bridge

This spring saw the deaths of four wildland firefighters in Colorado. A SEAT (Single Engine Air Tanker) pilot, a water tender driver and two firemen driving through dense smoke all perished. Each tragic death meant wives, children and loved ones were left behind.

The two men driving through the smoke were experienced fire personnel attempting to save the lives and property of their friends and neighbors. They had probably driven the road numerous times. But this time, as they crossed a flame weakened bridge, it suddenly collapsed beneath them, hurling them to their deaths.

This tragedy should cause all of us to rethink our approach when driving through smoke, fog or other poor visibility settings.

What about during the "smoky" times of our lives? When our marriage, finances or career, seems to be going up in smoke. What's going to hold us up? Are the "bridges" we're depending on strong enough to carry us through?

As much as they love us, family and friends alone aren't always enough. Fortunately, there is a God who loves us and wants to bring us safely over these burning bridges of life. As Romans 5:8 tells us, "But God demonstrates His own love for us in this: while we were still sinners, Christ died for us."

My old coffee-drinking buddy, Charles Spurgeon, used to say, "Even when you can't see the hand of God, you can trust the heart of God."

Jesus calls out to each of us, "Come to me, all you who are weary and burdened, and I will give you rest" (Matthew 11:28). In other words, He really is our "Bridge over troubled waters."

✝

Cry Out to Jesus!

It was a rough spring to say the least. Things started looking bad in January when I discovered a problem with my knee that would require surgery. Not good news for a wildland firefighter. In February I received word from the doctor that I had prostate cancer; curable but surgery would be required and a loss of income. In March our only grandson perished in a car wreck. In April my wife was diagnosed with blood clots in her lungs, you get the picture.

Have you ever felt that things were becoming "hopeless"? That the fire, finances or marriage were beyond hope? Often it's something we couldn't prevent; a wind shift, loss of job, etc. Other times it was the result of poor choices or sin on our part. Whatever the cause, the result can be the same, a feeling of hopelessness.

"You believe that there's nothing and there is no one who can make it right?" [1]

So how do you respond to hopelessness? Do you become hyper-active, trying to be too busy to think about the situation. Or do you try to drown your despair with alcohol or the abuse of drugs. Some even take the ultimately selfish step of taking their life; not realizing that it's a "permanent solution to a temporary problem" which hurts the very ones who love them.

The wonderful news of Jesus is that He brings hope to the hopeless! Jesus told us that the devil is a thief whose aim is to steal, kill and destroy; while Jesus came to give us an abundant life! (John 10) That abundant life includes helping us through times that seem hopeless. No, He doesn't always make the trials go away, but He always walks with us through the trials. In fact, those are the times that His help can be felt strongest, if we will receive it; if we will turn to Him in faith. Jesus makes a wonderful offer to us; "Come to me, all you who are weary and burdened, and I will give you rest" (Matthew 11:28).

In the midst of this turbulent time, as Melva and I were leaving a church service, a song began to play. Its lyrics became very important to us!

> There is hope for the helpless [1]
> Rest for the weary
> And love for the broken heart
> And there is grace and forgiveness
> Mercy and healing
> He'll meet you wherever you are
> Cry out to Jesus

So what happened? My knee surgery went well and I'm still passing the pack test. I went to Atlanta for prostate surgery and was picked up at the airport hotel by the "Grace of God Taxi Service." (No kidding, I have the pictures!) Two months later I was on fires in MT. The Lord gave us grace through the assurance of our grandson's place in heaven, and my wife's blood clots disappeared over the next few months. We're learning that His grace is sufficient for every need we have when we draw close to Him.

"May the God of *hope* fill you with all joy and peace as you trust in him, so that you may overflow with *hope* by the power of the Holy Spirit" Romans 15:13 (italics mine).

[1] Cry Out to Jesus by Third Day

CHAPTER NINE

Lessons Learned
on the Fireline

"Then I will pour out my thoughts to you, I will make known to you my teachings."

Proverbs 1:23b

Wildland Firefighters' Guide to the Christian Life

"Helicopter 5 Charlie Hotel, we could sure use your help on this spot fire."

"Affirmative, I'll bring in the bucket as low as I can. Be sure you get your people back out of the way."

During fifty seasons of wildland firefighting, I have noticed that we use many Christian principles in our standard operating procedures or protocol. Unfortunately, we in the church often forget these protocols, even though the Bible clearly teaches them. Take a look and see if you agree.

The Incident Commander and the Overhead Team. On every wildland fire, one of the first things we do is appoint someone as the Incident Commander. This person is usually the most experienced person on the scene. Their job isn't to do all the work, but rather to coordinate our efforts. They help train and equip us and oversee the work on the fire.

Isn't this what the Bible tells us in Ephesians 4:11-12? That God appoints leaders in the church to help equip and train us to do the work of the Kingdom of God. We can't sit back and rely on the pastor to do the work. We are to report for duty and use our particular gifts under his leadership.

The first thing an effective Incident Commander does is to assemble an overhead team. Recognizing that some people are stronger in certain areas, he or she appoints someone as operations chief, another as safety officer, and so on. In the Scriptures we read that each Christian receives gifts from God to help the whole church (1 Corinthians 12:7-11). The wise pastor-Incident Commander gathers around him a team of those gifted individuals and encourages them to function in their areas of strength.

Incident Objectives. Every briefing on a wildland fire incident begins with a review of our objectives. They generally start with, "To provide for public and firefighter safety," "To prevent the loss of structures," and so on. Each of us commits ourselves daily to these objectives. It often impresses me that people who don't normally get along, pull together to accomplish the objective of putting the fire out safely.

Yet, doesn't it seem that sometimes in our personal and church life we forget our Lord's objectives? Jesus said that we were to "Love the Lord your God with all your heart and with all your soul and with all your mind and with all your strength... (and) 'Love your neighbor as yourself." (Mark 12:30-31). And as a result, to "Therefore go and make disciples of all nations, baptizing them in the name of the Father and of the Son and of the Holy Spirit" (Matthew 28:19-20). What would happen if every day we reaffirmed our Lord's objectives?

Multiple Agency Response and Plain Text. On any major wildfire, a number of different agencies come together to put the fire out. It isn't unusual for Forest Service, Bureau of Land Management, Bureau of Indian Affairs, state and local fire districts, and many more to all participate. In order for us to work together effectively, we submit ourselves to the Incident Command System (ICS). The ICS sets up a unified chain of command with certain protocols.

One of the most important of these protocols is "plain text." In other words, we avoid the use of codes and buzz words that others on the fire may not be familiar with. Can you imagine the confusion that may ensue when someone on the fire hears over the radio, "10-76 on your 10-99?" (I actually heard a firefighter say that once. There was a pause and the person being addressed asked, "What's a 10-76?" Another pause and the first person said, "I don't know, what's a 10-99?")

In following our Lord's command to reach the world, we need to work together with other Christians. We need to put aside minor differences about styles of worship and denominational distinctions and focus on our mission. As we do so, let's use "plain text," especially when we share with those who aren't believers yet. As wonderful as being "justified by His vicarious and atoning sacrifice on our behalf that we may be consecrated to live sanctified lives" is, it might be more effective to say, "Jesus died so that we may live holy, forgiven and committed lives for Him."

Extreme Courtesy. One thing you will notice on a wildland fire is that there is unbelievable courtesy shown, especially on the radio. There's a lot of "Please" and "Thank you." The reason for this is twofold I believe. First, it helps prevent a panic sounding transmission. You think out your message and deliver it calmly. The second is that it takes into consideration the fact that the person on the other end may be going through all kinds of problems at the moment. They may be up to their armpits in alligators or, they may be exhausted from long, tiring days. A little courtesy goes a long way toward keeping a positive attitude.

In the same way, doesn't it help in our personal relationships and in our churches? We don't really know what the other person may be going through. By showing love and patience in our conversations, we build up one another (Romans 15:2).

The Task Book. On every wildland fire there are individuals working through their task books. A task book guides each firefighter through a series of training responsibilities he or she needs to go through before being "signed off" or qualified in certain positions. When done properly, this provides a strong mentoring experience that greatly enhances our learning. Sometimes, however, this process is abused by the mentor not taking the time to work through the task book with the trainee, or the trainee trying to "fast track" and avoid the training requirements. Both of these abuses not only shortchange the individual trainee, but ultimately hurt the overall fire program.

Jesus shows us true mentoring when He offers to yoke Himself together with us and teach us (Matthew 11:28). Paul mentored Timothy and encouraged him to do the same to other trustworthy individuals (2 Timothy 2:2). When we follow the Master's guidelines the church will truly be strong and growing.

Who really puts the fire out? Any experienced wildland firefighter knows that we really don't put out large wildfires. Yes, we work hard at saving lives, structures, and valuable watersheds. And our efforts do a lot of good. But ultimately, large fires don't go out until the Lord sends rain or snow, the humidity goes up, the temperature goes down, and the wind stops blowing.

In the same way, anyone who serves in the Lord's work knows that no matter how hard we plan and sacrifice, real success only comes from the miraculous touch of the Lord. As Scripture says, "Having begun by the Spirit are you now being perfected by the flesh" (Galatians 3:3 NASB). Why do we think that we can do the life changing ministry of Christ on our own?

What do you think? Are there some things we can learn from "life on the fire line?" Are there ways we can improve and be more effective in achieving our ultimate "Incident Commander's" objectives? Perhaps we need more than occasional bucket-drops of His love and power! Instead, we need to commit ourselves to do His work, His way, in the power of His Holy Spirit, and to His glory! Then we can take off our helmets at the end of the day and hear Him say, "Well Done."

✝

Billy Graham and the Fireman

On February 21, 2018 my close friend Billy Graham was "promoted to glory"! Ok, I only met Mr. Graham briefly a few times, but he was the type of man you felt was a "close friend" even if you never met him. After all, he was considered "America's Pastor" by Christians and non-Christians alike.

Billy Graham never served as a fireman, yet he appeared in support of first responders at numerous disasters including the 1995 Oklahoma City bombing and his Rapid Response Chaplains have served at Ground Zero as well as fires, hurricanes and disasters. In fact, one of his chaplains led my co-worker Craig to Christ in the recent California wildfires.

What made Billy Graham so special? USA today may have hit it on the head when they said he was "An Unspectacular Preacher Preaching a Spectacular Gospel." Larry Ross, who worked with Mr. Graham for over 30 years said, "People often ask me what one word describes Billy Graham's distinctive witness. I have to use three: faithfulness (to his calling,) authenticity (the same person one-an-one as in the pulpit) and integrity (doing the right thing, beyond doing things right)." Many times, I heard his closest co-workers say he was the humblest man they'd ever been with.

So, the question arises, when we answer our last tone-out, what will be our legacy? What will our family and those closest to us say about us? Will it be faithfulness, authenticity and integrity; or faithlessness, inauthentic and lack of integrity? Will they comment on our humility or say we were self-absorbed? Did our lives reflect a belief that we must decrease and Christ must increase (John 3:30)?

Before we are consumed by the fires of condemnation, stand down. We aren't finished! We still have time to rewrite our legacy. It's not too late! When we received Jesus as our Savior and Lord He sent the Holy Spirit to live in us. This third person of the Trinity has many functions but one major one is to remake us into the image of Christ (2 Corinthians 3:18).

None of us are too old, too ingrained, that He cannot transform us. All it takes is for us to humble ourselves and yield to the Spirit's work each day. He'll start as soon as we let Him. Sure, just like our rookie training there will be a series of successes and stumbling. Sometimes it will seem like we're not making any progress, but we are! Every day we read God's word and yield to His Spirit is another step forward.

Billy Graham would be the first to tell you of his times of struggle and mistakes, but he would also tell each of us to get up and keep moving forward. To finish strong!

†

Where's Bob?

"Where's Bob?" I called on the radio. No one seemed to know. My engine crew was "bumping hose" up a hillside in California in support of a Hotshot Crew's burnout and one of my crew was missing. It was a hot, dry, steep hillside and the hose lays were heavy. Had Bob tripped and hurt himself? Was he having a medical emergency? Immediately we ceased moving hose and began searching for Bob.

I had just been detailed in as the engine captain from my home Forest in Colorado. Bob was on my engine, I was responsible for him and he was missing. Has that ever happened to you?

In Luke chapter 15, Jesus tells of a shepherd losing a sheep and how he left the ninety-nine others to search until he found it. Then He tells of a young man who deliberately "wandered off." We see the Father looking down the road, waiting for the son to return. As we read, we begin to see the point; we see that the Shepherd/Father is God, the wayward sheep/wayward son is us! Even if we have deliberately wandered away, which we all have, the stories tell us that He still loves us! He is waiting for us to return, He even sends His Spirit to look for us. We are that important to Him!

But what should we do? When we realize we've wandered away from God, that we have sinned, what must we do? Should we try to hide? Would it be right for Bob to try to avoid the very folks that are trying to help him? God loves us so much that He sent His only Son, Jesus, to die in our place, to pay the death penalty for our sin. He then calls out to us to be rescued from sin and its consequences. Should we run away from the very One who came to save us? Shouldn't we cry out in response to His call and give our lives to Him?

After suspending our hose operation to search for Bob, which halted the burnout, one of the crew calls me on the radio. "Bob's ok. He decided to go back to the engine to drop off something and didn't bother to let anyone know." Along with the relief we all felt, there was a frustration that Bob hadn't thought of how his actions would affect me, his crew, and the Hot Shots waiting for hose. He had a role in the operation and was accountable to make sure we knew where he was at all times!

How about you and me? Do we realize that we're accountable to our brothers and sisters in Christ, and that when we "wander" away from the Lord it affects all of us? Have we given someone the right / the task of making sure we're staying accountable?

CHAPTER TEN

Believe and Receive

Making Eternal Decisions

"For God so loved the world that He gave His one and only Son, that whoever believes in Him shall not perish but have eternal life."

John 3:16

Did He Have a Bible?

The sickness had gone terribly bad; a 37-year fireman had died; leaving a wife, children and family grieving.

I was asked to conduct his funeral. He'd been involved in aircraft/fire/rescue in another city and I didn't know him well. Most of all I didn't know if he'd given his life to Jesus.

As I met with his family, I heard many great things about this man. He was a committed father, son and brother. He was working on restoring his marriage. He was well liked and respected in his profession. But the question remained; did he know Jesus, was he in heaven or hell?

So, I asked his children if their dad had a favorite Bible verse? "Yes," they replied, "John 3:16." Then I asked, "Did he have a Bible that I could use in the service?" Again, the answer was "yes"!

Imagine my joy when I opened the Bible and discovered it had been given to him when he had trusted Jesus as Savior and Lord, less than four years before!

I began to ask myself, when I die, what will help those left behind know where I am spending eternity? Will they find evidence that I loved Jesus and had committed my life to following Him? How about you?

†

She Survived an Entrapment But Died Anyway!

The messages came just days apart, a double whammy that stunned all of us on the fire line. Five wildland firefighters had died on duty in the western United States. Four perished in a helicopter crash in Idaho, another in a Utah burnover. All of us grieved over the loss and fire crews throughout the Great Basin stood down for an hour.

As I finished my fourteen-day rotation, I received a call from a Christian Hot Shot Superintendent. "Rick," he said, "one of the women who perished in the helo crash had just survived an entrapment on the Little Venus Fire."

Helicopter crashes on fires are very rare, and so is being entrapped during a burnover. Yet, this woman had experienced both within weeks. And the second time she perished.

What does that say to us? Does it remind us of Hebrews 9:27, "Just as people are destined to die once, and after that to face judgment," or Psalm 90:12, "Teach us to number our days..."? To me, it affirmed some things and left some hard questions.

It affirmed the fact that, yes, each one of us does have an appointment with death. To some, it may come in their nineties, others much, much younger. We need to be ready to meet God and His judgment at any moment.

The questions are haunting. Was this woman ready to face the judgment? Had someone shared with her the good news of salvation and forgiveness of sin? Had I met her? Had I been sensitive to live a godly example and share Jesus with her? Had her first encounter been a "wake-up call," another chance to come to Jesus?

None of us is promised another day, either to turn from sin and receive Christ, or to share with others the soul-saving message. Shouldn't we pray to the Father that we will be guided by the Holy Spirit and respond to Him every day, in every way?

When helicopter pilots leave the ground, they radio in the number of "souls on board" along with their destination and fuel supply.

God help us remember that there really are "souls on board" every incident.

✝

Prepare to Die

Twenty emergency services workers in Bay St. Louis, MS, realized that the time had come. They were about to die. Bay St. Louis is no stranger to hurricanes. But, with the exception of Camille in 1969, most had brought relatively limited damage. So, when forecasters warned that Katrina would hit within a few hours, a group of EMS workers volunteered to ride the storm out in order to render immediate aid when the storm passed.

The problem was, Katrina hit with unmatched fury. The storm surge reached higher and higher. Soon, the seriousness of their situation became apparent. As the first floor of the courthouse flooded they moved to the second. When the second floor flooded, they moved to the attic. Then, the water approached the thirty-foot level. The realization hit them that there was no hope of rescue and they prepared to die. Taking an indelible marker, each inscribed their social security number on their arms to aid in identifying their bodies. Then they took the American flag that had flown over the courthouse and wrote their names on it so that their relatives would know who had perished in the room. The flag was then nailed to the ceiling of the attic.

Death comes to each of us. It's been said, "We have a 100% chance of dying." Many of us don't have several hours' notice to contemplate our eternal future. We are caught in a moment and ushered either into heaven or hell. Are we prepared to die? How can we be? The Bible tells us that those who have Christ as their Savior and Lord have eternal life (in heaven) and those who don't perish (eternal punishment in hell) (1 John 5:12). We can be ready by humbling ourselves before God, confessing our sins to Him, trusting in Jesus' dying in our place to pay for our sins, and making Him Lord over our lives, 24/7.

So, what happened to the Bay St. Louis EMS workers? Miraculously, the waters stopped rising, the building held and they survived. The flag now resides in the Emergency Operations Center. Undoubtedly, the thoughts each one had that day will permeate their lives forever. What about us? When our time comes, will we be ready?

†

What Happened to All the Trees?

"It's off to Mississippi for hurricane duty," the dispatcher told me. "Better check your vaccinations."

"Well," I thought, "I did pray about my next assignment." Secretly I had hoped it would be on a forest fire somewhere away from the devastation of hurricane Katrina. But, I've learned that when I let the Lord guide me I end up in the most fulfilling assignments. After checking with the requesting unit, it was decided that I should drive the 1500 miles since flights and rental rigs were in short supply.

After loading my gear (and checking my vaccinations), I drove twenty-four hours to Laurel, MS to become the field Safety Officer for twenty saw teams clearing over 400 miles of roads and trails. As I approached the Incident Command Post I began to marvel at what I saw. No apparent flood damage, but thousands of trees blown down or snapped. Big trees, oaks and pine tossed into roads, houses, and power lines. There were literally thousands of them. Entire plantations of lumber producing trees turned into salvage sales.

I had loaded my Explorer with clothes and canned goods quickly gathered from our local churches (a semi-truck would follow later). As I unloaded the items at a local church, I saw busses and vans from churches around the country already arriving. Sawyers from CO, builders from SC, volunteers from CA and OK joining hands with the local believers to reach out in Jesus' love.

As is my custom, I began to make firefighter *Answering the Call* New Testaments available to my federal coworkers. Soon I ran out and had to start taking names. After shift on Sunday, I held a chapel service in the mess tent. Initially, only one person showed up, but then others joined in. One young man working with the camp crew received assurance of salvation. Later in the week a member of the overhead team asked how to know Christ and I was able to share the plan of salvation and pray with him.

After two weeks I was on my way home to Colorado. Again, the number of healthy trees destroyed by the wind overwhelmed me. I began to think of Jesus' words "Therefore everyone who hears these words of mine and puts them into practice is like a wise man who built his house on the rock. The rain came down, the streams rose, and the winds blew and beat against that house; yet it did not fall, because it had its foundation on the rock. But everyone who hears these words of mine and does not put them into practice is like a foolish man who built his house on sand. The rain came down, the streams rose, and the winds blew and beat against that house, and it fell with a great crash" (Matthew 7:24-27).

No matter how strong we look or feel, if we aren't building our house on the rock of Jesus and His Word, we too will be snapped when the winds blow.

†

Where's the Helicopter?!

Last summer, two wildland firefighters died as they vainly awaited a helicopter rescue. The two had been dropped off to build a
helispot which would be used to shuttle crews and supplies to the
head of the fire. Shortly after lunch, the fire began to increase in
intensity. Rather than move into a Safety Zone, the two continued
to work. They apparently were depending on the helicopter to return and remove them. They called on the radio repeatedly, but
no one came. Both ships were out of service at the heliport, miles
away, shut down with maintenance issues. When a ship was finally launched, it couldn't land because of heavy smoke. The two
firefighters perished, waiting for help that never came.

Recently, a man and woman died spiritually as they vainly
awaited their good works to save them. They had been placed on
earth to love and serve both God and man. Their life had deterio-
rated after they chose to disobey God. Rather than take refuge in
the Safety Zone of forgiveness prepared for them by Jesus Christ,
they continued to plug along on their own, trusting their good
works to eventually deliver them. The good works were never sufficient. They were plagued by maintenance problems (wrong motives, sin nature, etc). The man and woman perished, trusting in
themselves rather than Jesus.

In wildland firefighting, we know that air support is a fickle
lover. Just when we need them most, they're diverted to another
mission or down for maintenance. They are wonderful tools to
have, but you can't depend on them as your Escape Route or Safety Zone. In the same way, our good works are great to do, but they
will always let us down if we depend on them for salvation. We
can only be rescued by accepting God's gift of salvation. We do
this by entering into His Safety Zone of forgiveness. By placing
our trust in Jesus' death for our sins, trusting Him alone for salvation. Then we can be delivered from perishing and the fires of
hell. Don't wait too late; enter into His love, protection and salvation today! (2 Corinthians 6:1-2).

Whose Fault Was It, Really?

The fire crews are trapped, a critical weather warning doesn't reach the fire line and horrible deaths occur. Who's at fault? The crews? The weather forecaster? The dispatcher?

As a wildland firefighter and safety trainer, I review and analyze wildfire fatalities over and over. Seeking some sense of the cause of the tragedy, and most importantly, how to prevent another one from occurring.

As I studied fourteen deaths on Storm King Mountain in Colorado, something leaped out at me. I saw two terrible facts emerging. First, the firefighters on Storm King died because we broke our own rules. (I say "we" because as each of us is inextricably related to each other. We are family. If one suffers, we all suffer.) Yes, we broke our own rules. We built fireline downhill with fire below us. We failed to post lookouts. We didn't have adequate escape routes and safety zones. We didn't ask for weather forecasts. And, as a result of breaking the rules, fourteen of our family perished.

Second, a warning that would have given those on the mountain the opportunity and motivation to escape — a high wind warning for fifty mile-an-hour winds — was never delivered to the crews. If the message had been received, and acted on immediately, the crews could have escaped over the top of the ridge and survived.

So, whose fault was it, really? Ultimately, if we stand back and look at the tragedy, the fourteen died because they knowingly ignored and broke the standard safety rules that we train with every year. These, who were some of our brightest and best, our most experienced family members, knew they were "pushing the envelope." Yet, for some reason, no one sounded the alarm, called for an about face, until it was too late.

Does some responsibility also lay with those who failed to deliver the last-minute warning? — The warning that would hopefully have prompted the firemen and women to turn back while there was still time? Yes, of course.

What about the even greater tragedy of being overrun by the fires of eternal hell?

The Bible tells us repeatedly that there is a place of eternal punishment. A place where the "fire never goes out" and the "worm never dies." A place of torment and separation from God's love and all that is good. It also tells us that we go there because we break God's rules — rules that He has shown us in His Bible and in our own consciences — rules that we are all aware of.

It also tells us that God loves us so much that He doesn't want any of us to perish. He has provided an *Escape Route* to *His Safety Zone*, to Heaven. That *Escape Route* is Jesus. Jesus paid the price for our breaking God's rules by dying in our place on the cross. And, as the result of His death and resurrection, He has opened the way for us to be forgiven and escape God's judgment. If we'll turn around now, and heed His call, we will be spared. If we will confess to Him that we were wrong, trust Him to forgive us, and follow Him with all our heart and actions, we will go over the ridge before the flames reach us!

But what if the emergency message is not delivered? Whose fault is it then that millions perish? Ultimately, the fault lies with each of us who break God's rules. We have rebelled against Him and as a result are about to be overtaken by His just judgment. But, if His message of salvation isn't delivered by those of us who have received it, then we too are accountable in the eternal tragedy.

"Now as for you, son of man, I have appointed you a watchman ... so you will hear a message from my mouth and give them warning from Me. When I say to the wicked, 'o wicked man, you will surely die,' and you do not speak to warn the wicked from his way, that wicked man shall die in his iniquity, but his blood I will require from your hand" (Ezekiel 33:7-8 NASB).

✝

Escape To ... ?

"Run for your lives!!" came the call as hundreds of wildland fire-fighters were caught in a series of huge blowups. It was mid-August, 1910. The northwest United States was a tinderbox. Hurricane force winds pushed each new start into massive crown fires. Crews were trapped, blinded by smoke and flames. Where could they run? Where could they find shelter?

Each of us faces infernos in our lives. The impending collapse of a marriage, financial ruin, or the death of a loved one; and the infernos often come with hurricane force. Where can we run to? Where can we find shelter? Sadly, some seek to escape into the "box canyon" of alcohol and drugs; only to find there's no exit. Others run into "chimneys" of immorality and pornography to be overcome by the smoke and heat of sin. Even more tragically, some leap into the flames of suicide. Each of these paths leads not only to self-destruction, but harm the lives of our loved ones as well.

Where can we run? The Bible tells us that God Himself is our refuge and strength, an ever-present help in time of trouble (Psalm 46:1). He calls us to run to Him when we are hurting (Matthew 11:28). In the midst of our infernos we are tempted to try to outrun the flames; even though our training tells us to follow our escape route to our safety zone. But trying to run away almost always brings disaster! We must run to Jesus in prayer, trusting Him to shield us; to preserve us and our families.

During the horrific firestorm of 1910, seventy-six firefighters and eight civilians perished. Only a heaven-sent storm of rain and snow slowed the three-million-acre conflagration. In the midst of the panic-filled day, Ranger Ed Pulaski was able to gather together 45 of his 150 men and at gunpoint herd them into a cave where he kept them all night. They survived. Pulaski became a wildland fire legend.

Where will you run? Where will you lead those around you? Now is the time to plan your escape route and safety zone! The blow-ups and inferno will come and it will take all our strength and discipline to run to Jesus and not be lured into false paths which lead only to destruction.

†

Reflections on John 3:16
From a Firefighter's Perspective

"For God so loved the world"
>A firefighter serves because he/she cares for people.
>God loves us with more love than we can ever imagine.

"That He gave"
>A firefighters gives of his/her time, strength, and sometimes even of his or her life for others.
>God loves us so much that He gave His own Son's life, for us!

"His one and only Son"
>Jesus, God's only Son, willingly gave His life to pay sin's death penalty for everyone of us.

"So that whosoever"
>A firefighter goes to the aid of all in need.
>God's offer of forgiveness is for all who come to Jesus!

"Believes in Him"
>A firefighter has to place their trust in their fellow fire fighters, equipment, etc.
>God calls us to place our trust, believe in, cling to, and rely upon Jesus to forgive our sin.

"Shall not perish"
>Unless a firefighter follows safety protocols, they eventually get seriously injured, or die.
>The Bible tells us that we have sinned and rebelled against God, and we will perish and spend eternity in hell. But Jesus promised that those who believe in Him will not perish!

"But have everlasting life"
>Those who place their lives in Jesus' hands will have everlasting, eternal life in heaven!

Souls on Board

When an aircraft leaves in route to a forest fire, the pilot tells the dispatcher his aircraft identification number, how long he estimates the flight will take, how long the fuel he has on board should last, and how many "souls on board."

We must realize that each of us as firefighters, spouses, and parents have "souls on board" in our life.

In fact, each of us has a soul and how we respond to Jesus' offer of salvation determines the safety of our soul. This is why John 3:16 is so important to each of us.

Have you asked God for forgiveness for your sin, trusting in Jesus' death in your place?

Have you yielded your life to Him as your Lord? Will you right now?

A simple prayer from your heart is sufficient.

> *"Lord Jesus, I am a sinner. I ask You to forgive me on the basis that You died on the cross to pay in full the price for my sin. I yield my life to You to be my Lord and my Savior. Please fill me with Your Holy Spirit each day and help me follow You. I trust You to do this because Your Bible promises You will forgive me and give me eternal life. Thank You!"*

Email me or write me if you have prayed that prayer. We have complimentary easy to read Bibles and other resources to send you which will help you get started in your new life. We want to help!

Now, start your new assignment as a "soul on board" with Jesus! Get a Bible you can read and understand. Start reading right away and every day; a good place to start is the book of John or Mark in the New Testament. Ask around and find a good church where the Bible is taught. Call the pastor; tell him you've given your life to Jesus. Explain your crazy work schedule and ask what meetings would be best for you. Start talking to God all through the day. Share everything with Him!

**May the Lord richly bless you and protect you.
See you on the "Big One"!**

Meet the Author

Rick Barton has been involved in wildland firefighting for over fifty years, working for the United States Forest Service, National Park Service, Colorado State Forest Service and Bureau of Land Management. He has served on hand-crews as Crew Boss, Engine Foreman, Strike Team Leader, Line Safety Officer and Public Information Officer.

Rick became a follower of Jesus while a student at Western State Colorado University and has served in various ministry roles including holding chapels on firelines since then. Rick and his wife Melva still live in Gunnison, Colorado, have been married for almost fifty years and have four adult children. He holds graduate degrees from Wheaton College, Denver Seminary and Southern Seminary.

Books and Posters Available from

Rick Barton Ministries
PO Box 1155
Gunnison, CO 81230

email: *barton@gunnison.com*

RickBartonMinistries.org

Made in the USA
Columbia, SC
27 January 2019